SUGINO YOSHIO

THE LITTLE GIANT OF MODERN JAPAN'S MARTIAL ARTS

CHRISTOPHER M. CLARKE

Cover photo: Sugino Yoshio (1904-1998).

© 2014 Christopher M. Clarke, Clarke's Canyon Press, Huntingtown, MD 20639.

TABLE OF CONTENTS

Foreword	5
Sugino Yoshio	7
Sugino's Youth	9
Shingai Tadatsu	10
From college student to *judo* champion	11
Iizuka Kunisaburo	12
Toku Sambo	16
Adding *jujutsu* and *aikido*	20
Yoshin Koryu Jujutsu	21
Taking up the sword	28
Tenshin Shoden Katori Shinto-ryu	29
Tenshin Shoden Katori Shinto-ryu Lineage	33
Katori Shrine	34
Futsunushi-no-mikoto	34
Connections and Descendant Schools	35
Tenshin Shoden Katori Shinto-ryu Curriculum	37
Teaching and healing during the War	40
Sugino: Behind-the-scenes movie star	43
Decades of dedication	46
Sugino Yoshio's Personality	48
Questions about Sugino's "legitimacy"	52
Preface to Sugino's 1941 *Tenshin Shoden Katori Shinto-ryu Budo Kyohan*	54
Postscript	57
Notes	61

FOREWORD

Sugino Yoshio (杉野嘉男, December 12, 1904-June 13, 1998) was one of—if not the—most accomplished, widely and deeply trained martial artists of the 20th century. A top student of *kenjutsu, judo, aikido* and numerous classical weapons, he was also one of the most beloved and respected *budo* masters in Japan. Yet his story is barely known in the West.

Sugino actually started his formal martial arts career relatively late. Although he was known for loving to participate in mock "sword fights" as a youngster, it was not until he reached college that he first began real training. He quickly became a *judo* champion, opening a *dojo* with Master Kano Jigoro's approval at the age of only 22, undoubtedly one of the youngest people Kano ever sanctioned to teach on his own.

At Kano's suggestion, Sugino took up studying one of the few remaining classical *jujutsu* styles, eventually reaching *kyoshi* level. At about the same time, and also at Kano's recommendation, he began training in *Tenshin Shoden Katori Shinto-ryu*, one of the few surviving truly ancient styles of *hyogo* (the arts of war), which included a huge curriculum of weapons, unarmed combat, military strategy and other subjects.

Despite his already sterling credentials and accumulated martial knowledge, Sugino was not yet content that he had plumbed the depths of Japanese *budo*. At the age of about 27, he enrolled as a student of Ueshiba Morihei, the founder of *Aikido* and a well-known and widely respected martial artist. In fact, Sugino was one of several of Kano's most promising students that the founder of *judo* sent to Ueshiba to round out his art. After less than five years, Ueshiba issued Sugino a teaching license and asked him to become a full-time *aikido* teacher.

Somewhere in this whirlwind of martial activity, Sugino also found time to become a qualified bone-setter, a type of medicine that many martial arts masters pursued both for income and to attend to training injuries among their students.

For the next 60 years, Sugino was a fixture on the Japanese martial arts stage, teaching in a number of locations, training *uchi deshi* (live-in pupils), and often being called on to demonstrate his art at major national venues. He may best be remembered, however, for having choreographed the weaponry fighting scenes for several of the classic movie collaborations between director Akira Kurosawa and actor Toshiro Mifune, including the famous duel against seven opponents in the 1956 movie, "The Seven Samurai."

In 1995, at the age of 91, Sugino traveled to France, one of several countries where he had long-time students, and presented a demonstration that showed his extraordinary vitality and captivated his audience. Sugino continued to teach until shortly before his death in 1998, leaving his *dojo* and style to his son, Sugino Yukihiro. At only 5'2" and about 120 pounds, Sugino was truly the little giant of 20th century Japan's martial arts.

SUGINO YOSHIO

SUGINO'S YOUTH

Sugino Yoshio was born in Naruto, a farming village in coastal Japan just north of Tokyo on December 12, 1904. The head of his family had served for generations as the head of the village, and in former times may have been *jizamurai* or *goshi*, "samurai of the land," or low-level warriors who farmed but would be called up for military service in the event that their lord went to war. From the beginning of the Tokugawa period, the family was accorded the privilege of having a surname and wearing a sword, privileges not allowed to commoners.[1]

Yoshio was small for his age and full of energy. While still young, his parents moved to Tokyo and enrolled him at the age of six in an elementary school. Strangely, given his later devotion to traditional Japanese martial arts, he created something of a stir on his first day in school by showing up in Western-style clothing rather than the traditional Japanese garb that was expected. His father was strict, inculcating an ethos of hard work and honesty in young Yoshio, apparently sometimes by means of corporal punishment. As a result, Yoshio grew up "with a good deal of fortitude and always kept a stiff upper lip…[he was] quite imperturbable."[2] Not very interested in his studies, Yoshio preferred staging mock sword fights with his peers, and became rather a leader in creating mischief.

According to one account, he was introduced to *kendo* at the age of 12 under the tutelage of Shingai Tadatsu, a *hanshi* under the *Butokukai*[3] in *Tamiya-Shingen-ryu kenjutsu*.[4] (See next page.) Sugino apparently did not take to *kendo* at this time.

Despite his apparent lack of interest in his studies, Sugino must have been bright. He not only entered primary school a year early, but in 1918, at the age of 14, Sugino entered the Department of Commerce and Industry of Keio University.[5] He thrived in that atmosphere; students were required to join at least one extracurricular club and attend weekly, but Sugino joined virtually every club available.

"I was in just about every club there was," he recalls, "*judo, kendo, kyudo, sumo* and quite a few others. I'd join just about anything I was asked to." He was particularly active in the

SHINGAI TADATSU

Shingai, a former *samurai*, was a member of the Imperial Household staff and in 1886 was hired as one of the sword-fighting instructors of the newly established police force.[6] Although one source says he held the equivalent of a *yodan* (fourth degree), this is somewhat misleading.[7] Shingai was a major figure in the modernization of *kendo*, although not among the first *kenshi* [swordsmen] awarded top rank by the *Butokukai*.[8] He likely was ranked *kyoshi*, the level just below *hanshi* (master) by around the turn of the century. In 1906, he appears to have been a member of the committee that created the short-lived *Keishicho Gekken Kata* (Police Sword-fighting Form).[9] In 1911—when Sugino was about seven years old—Shingai was a *hanshi* and one of 25 members of the *Butokukai* committee formed to create a unified *kendo kata*.[10] (Of the 25, only five, including Shingai, were *hanshi*.) Shingai was a master of the *Tamiya-Shinken-ryu* style of *iaido* and the only member of his style on the committee). The *Tamiya-ryu* was founded by Tamiya Heibei Shigemasa (田宮平兵衛, c. 1590), a direct student of Hayashizaki Jinsuke Shigenobu (林崎 甚助 重信, 1542-1621) who is often considered the founder of *iaido*.[11] The style, dating back some 400 years, consisted of three sets of *kata*, one with 11 techniques, one with 14 techniques, and a two-person set of seven techniques with the long sword (*tachi*) and three with the short sword (*wakizashi*).

boating club and in some clubs that would be inconceivable in Japan today, such as the pistol club. "I remember shooting at a pigeon in the schoolyard, but I missed," he says.[12]

While in college, Sugino may have continued to study *kendo* under *Hanshi* Shingai—the sources are somewhat confusing—but he reportedly showed little aptitude and made little progress. Undoubtedly, this study consisted primarily of *shinai kendo* competition. It is doubly ironic, then, that Sugino was soon to become a top competitor in *judo* and was to devote his life to studying and teaching a *koryu* (ancient style) of *kenjustu*, albeit one in which complex and difficult two-man *kata* performed with *bokken* (wooden swords) or *shinken* (real swords) are the heart of the system, rather than competition with *shinai* (bamboo swords) and *bogu* (armor). After training for a while, Sugino gave up *kendo* to concentrate on *judo*.

FROM COLLEGE STUDENT TO JUDO CHAMPION

At Keio, Sugino found his first love: *judo*. And little wonder: the "vertically challenged" Sugino was to study under one of Kano Jigoro's top students, Iizuka Kunisaburo, 8th *dan*, and a man even shorter than Sugino. (See next page.) Sugino began training every morning and evening, "his desire to strengthen himself leading him to spend more time on the mat than anyone else."[13] The Keio *judo* club was not considered a powerhouse, although under Iizuka's strict training it was beginning to improve.

One time, while Sugino was a student, Keio was to participate in a *judo* tournament with the four-school alliance comprised of Kuramae Engineering University, Tokyo University of Agriculture, Rissho University, and Tokyo University of Fisheries.

> The Keio team being short on members, Iizuka arranged for Sugino to participate despite the fact that he was still only a first *kyu*. His opponents were all huge black belts. But Sugino stepped onto the mat wearing his brown belt and threw his way through six of them, with the seventh match ending in a draw. Afterward his teammates crowded around him congratulating him: "You're so small, but you fought so well in there! Even Iizuka *Sensei* thought so." He came away from the tournament with unprecedented new confidence.[14]

At the end of the year Sugino took his *shodan* exam at the Kodokan on Iizuka's recommendation. "This time he defeated six opponents in a row, earning for himself the rank of '*shodan* with honors' [*batsugun shodan*], a rank which existed at that time and indicated performance above and beyond that required for an ordinary *shodan*."[15]

Sugino continued training hard, constantly experimenting on ways that a smaller man could defeat a larger opponent: there were no weight divisions in *judo* tournaments at the time. Over the next several years, he devised methods of using *urawaza* (rear techniques, presumably including sacrifice throws) and *kaeshiwaza* (reversals). From that time until he earned his 4th *dan* in 1928, Sugino remained undefeated.

IIZUKA KUNISABURO

Iizuka Kunisaburo (1875-1958) started learning *jujutsu* at the age of 14 at the Keio Gijuku (later Keio University), but his study was interrupted the following year when he went off to attend a naval academy in Tokyo. There was no *judo* or *jujutsu* class at the academy, but one day "he saw a man carrying a *judo* uniform and followed him to the Kodokan. There he applied for entry, was found acceptable, and signed its enrollment book on November 23, 1891. In his first bout with a much larger and more experienced black belt, he was thrown about. 'As I was a rather pretentious young man I was burning with rage,' Iizuka later recalled. 'In order not to be beaten by him and to beat him, I applied myself very seriously to my work.'"[16]

Short, but "built on the lines of a mini-Hercules," Iizuka thrived in *judo* competition.[17] By 1905—after only 14 years of training—Iizuka had reached the rank of 6th *dan*. He first served as assistant instructor at the "Tokyo Advanced Teachers Training School and at the Seventh Senior High School Zoshikan (in Kagoshima). Beginning from 1899, he spent 7 years in Fukuoka as a [ordained Shinto] priest at the Fukuoka Prefectural Shuyukan Senior High School, as a part-time employee of the Fukuoka Teachers Training School, and as the Tenshikan master."[18]

After the Russo-Japanese War, Iizuka hoped to be selected in 1906 for an overseas assignment by the Kodokan to teach *judo*, but instead accepted a teaching job at his alma mater, now Keio University. He served there for 38 years (until 1945), turning Keio into a *judo* powerhouse, and remaining affiliated with the school until his death in 1958. He was widely considered the leading collegiate *judo* coach of the 1930s and was one of the first people promoted to 10th *dan*. "He also served as master at the Imperial Fisheries Institute, and at the Tokyo Institute of Technology, while at the same time opening the Itogokan *dojo* in Shibuya where he taught *Judo*. Mr. Iizuka died on July 25, 1958 at the age of 84."[19]

Event	Date
Enters Kodokan	November 1891
Shodan	September 1893
Nidan	January 1895
Sandan	April 1896
Yodan	January 1899
Godan	August 1901
Rokudan	June 1908
Nanadan	January 1916
Hachidan	February 1922
Kudan	December 1937
Judan	May 1946

He looked back on that period in an interview with *Aikido* instructor and historian Stanley Pranin in 1985:

> In 1922 I received my *shodan* in *Judo*. It was what we called a "*batsugun shodan*" (distinguished shodan) awarded to those with excellent records. Probably you are not familiar with the term. In my day, military officers, Tokujiro Akagawa and Kunijiro Minagawa also became "*batsugun shodan*". Mr. Akakawa threw about 12 or 13 people and Mr. Minagawa threw about 16. If you were a *batsugun shodan* you were treated differently from normal *shodan*. People tended to regard you as a cut above the others. After I became *shodan* I was never defeated in the "*Kohaku jiai*" (a contest or tourney between two groups) whose records are preserved in the Kodokan. I would always throw my opponents and in this way was elevated to 4th *dan*...
>
> Weight divisions were introduced after the war... Although I was very small I was strong and was never defeated. There was a particular match I had when I was a 4th *dan* that I consider my best one. At that time those who were ranked 5th *dan* didn't participate in matches any more. The highest rank for competition was 4th *dan*... Since I was young then I was pretty conceited.[20]

Sugino was clearly one of *judo*'s up-and-comers. One of his contemporaries—Mochizuki Minoru, who was one grade behind Sugino in *judo*—later remarked, "Sugino? That guy has the *kami* [divine] in him!"[21] Sugino "always exploited openings left by opponents who carelessly underestimated him because of his small size. But more than anything he had the confidence that his teacher Iizuka had planted in him."[22]

As one of *judo*'s rising stars, Sugino drew the attention of the Kodokan's top officials, including Dr. Kano himself. On September 15, 1925—still only 22 years old—Sugino was given permission to open his own *dojo* (which included a bone setting clinic) in Kawasaki City. Sugino later remarked that "Teachers today may not be aware of it, but at that time unless an instructor was a 3rd *dan* or higher he was not allowed to establish a branch *dojo* of the Kodokan. Also, we were obliged to report to the Kodokan the number of new students and total practitioners and the amount of fees we received every month."[23] Sugino also grew his later-trademark beard at the time because he had trouble being taken seriously as a martial arts teacher because he looked so young.

Kano some time before had concluded that the Kodokan's mission should include not only spreading his new and "modern" *judo*, but helping to preserve the traditional martial arts, lest they disappear altogether.[24] Kano had extensive and friendly relations with numerous masters of traditional martial arts from his role as an official at the *Butokukai*; he even attempted to recruit Funakoshi Gichin to teach the newly introduced art of Okinawan *karate* at the Kodokan, but Funakoshi declined, fearing that he would lose his independence and that his art would be subsumed under the rapidly popularizing art of *judo*.

As a result of his preservation efforts, Kano invited a number of masters of traditional *koryu* to teach senior students at the Kodokan and encouraged his most promising students to take up at least one of the traditional systems. After Sugino earned his 4th *dan*, Kano told him that he should consider taking up one of the traditional *kobujutsu* in addition to his *judo*. This was not unusual. Mochizuki Minoru later remembered:

> I had been staying at Mifune [Kyuzo] *Sensei*'s home all this time and I too felt the need to engage in spiritual training and so I joined the research group. At that time I was also a second degree black belt in *kendo* so I already understood how to use the sword, the footwork, and how to extend my arms. So I was completely different from those teachers who had done only *judo*. That's why after I started to take part in training in the classical arts I came to the attention of Kano *Sensei*. "You have the makings of a leader," he told me. After that I was to report to him once or twice a month on the progress of my training. While I was doing that *Sensei* said to me one day, "In the future you will be a top teacher here at the Kodokan." I was stunned. At that time among the teaching greats were Mifune *Sensei* and Tokusanbo *Sensei*. I wondered if I could ever reach such heights.[25]

No doubt, Kano had similar conversations with Sugino and monitored his progress with similar meetings.

TOKU SAMBO

Mifune Kyuzo, the genius of *judo*, need little introduction.[26] The "Tokusanbo" Sugino trained with, however, is virtually unknown outside of *judo* historians' circles. Some say he was an Okinawan who taught both *judo* and some form of *karate*, but historian John Stevens says he was from southern Kagoshima prefecture.[27] It is possible that, like many other Okinawans, he had moved to Japan to seek work or training. Mochizuki put him on the same plane as Mifune, saying that "In those days in judo circles they said, 'For technique, it's Mifune but the devil of the Kodokan is Tokusanbo.'"[28] Toku Sampo was said to be "The Epitome of *Judo Randori*," according to Mochizuki.[29]

Nevertheless, like a few of Kano's other most promising students, Toku Sambo (or Sampo, 1887-1945) had a penchant for constantly getting in fights and trouble. According to historian John Stevens, after being fired from several jobs and expelled from the Kodokan,

Toku ended up back in Kagoshima, where he enlisted in the military as a member of a gunnery squad. Although it is hard to believe, Toku got into a fight with an ornery stallion used to pull the cannons. The horse kicked Toku in the side, breaking two of his ribs. Toku replied with a punch to the horse's mouth that knocked the animal out. Toku's injury was so serious he was hospitalized for two months and then discharged from the military for reasons of health.[30]

Toku Sampo at age 26.

After a lengthy pilgrimage in the mountains, Toku eventually got himself under control and was readmitted to the Kodokan. In 1930, at the age of 45 and recuperating from pneumonia, Toku lost his first public bout, shocking his admirers. "Toku's loosing it," the rumor went. The next year, however, Toku threw seven opponents in a row, ranging from third to sixth *dan*, showing everyone that Toku "still had it."[31]

Toku's end was tragic. In the account of John Stevens:

> Toku died during the Tokyo air raid on March 10,1945. It is said that he and his wife drowned in the Sumida River while trying to save the children who had jumped into the water to avoid the flames. Toku was promoted to eighth dan in 1937 and ninth dan posthumously upon his death in 1945. Together with Saigo and Mifune, Toku is one of the great Kodokan legends.[32]

The Hall of Judo Luminaries at the Kodokan's Judo Museum and Library displays photographs and brief biographies of nineteen individuals who made significant contributions to the early teaching and development of judo. Ninth *dan* Sampo Toku, admired as "a lone cedar standing in the field" for his remarkable height and unbreakable good training posture is one of the 19.[33]

Mifune Kyuzo (left) with Kano.

Sugino's training was interrupted briefly by a foray into business. At the age of 20, soon after graduating from Keio University's Department of Commerce and Industry, Sugino accepted a lucrative position at the Taipei, Taiwan headquarters of a Japanese bank. (Since 1895, Taiwan had been under Japanese occupation.) He had hoped to use the position as a jumping off point to land a job in the bank's Singapore office where he could enjoy the temperate climate.[34] During his stay in Taipei, he trained for three hours every morning before work and participated vigorously in the local meets and tournaments. But an incident during a match there began to undermine his enthusiasm for *judo*:

> In May 1923 Sugino entered a *judo* competition in Taipei. He was selected as the first of five opponents to go against a third-*dan judoka* in a five-player elimination match. *Judoka* capable of making it through this sort of elimination competition are generally viewed as among the most skilled, with impressive strength and the ability to down at least five opponents in a match without too much difficulty. Perhaps deceived by Sugino's small stature, the third-*dan* moved in to execute what he probably thought would be an easy inner-thigh reap, but at the last instant Sugino caught him with a lightning-fast *utsurigoshi* (hip shift), one of his favorite techniques. The throw had been nearly perfect, but it so surprised the referee that he became confused as to how to call it. He hesitated to stop the match since the player still had four opponents to go. Wondering why the referee had said nothing, Sugino continued the match and brought the third-*dan* to the mat in a strangle hold. Eventually, his opponent tapped out in submission, but the referee ignored this as well. Having no other choice, Sugino continued to apply the technique until the poor fellow lost consciousness.[35]

Sugino was appalled at the result and felt shamed, as if he had been forced to do something dishonorable. He began to wonder about the objectiveness of *judo*'s technique and competitive atmosphere. These doubts were reinforced one day around five years later, when Sugino was discussing *judo* with a "nephew" of Kano "named Honda."* Sugino reportedly asked Honda:

---

* I have found no record of a "nephew" of Kano named Honda. Kano had two nephews named Nangu Saburo (1879-?) and Nango Jiro, (1876-1951) who began studying with Kano in *judo*'s early years. Jiro received his (continued)

whether *judo* had any secret principles (*gokui*), to which Honda replied that it did not. Sugino pressed the issue, asking again, "Really? None at all?" Honda reiterated his answer, saying no, none at all[:] Kodokan judo had no *gokui* nor any other secrets. "No *gokui*..." Sugino considered this deeply. Even games like *go* (a board game) and *shogi* (Japanese chess) had *gokui*; how could it possibly be that a *bujutsu*, an activity where one's very life was at stake, had none? It didn't make sense. "If *judo* has no *gokui*," Sugino reflected, "is it really worth practicing."[36]

Nango Jiro

This, combined with Sugino's continued dissatisfaction with the arbitrariness of contest judging led his enthusiasm for *judo* to wane. Although he continued to teach *judo* in his *dojo*, he increasingly began to seek other training to answer his nagging doubts.

---

black belt in 1884, while at the same time continuing a career in the navy, from which he retired as a rear admiral. When Kano died in 1938, the Kodokan board of trustees unanimously chose Jiro as his successor, a post he held until September, 1946, when he retired due to bad health. While president he established a system of *judo* for juveniles, fixed the *kata* and self-defense curriculum for women, and founded the institute for the training of teachers of *judo*. He was one of the few *judan*, 10th degree black belts promoted. Sugino may have confused Nango with Honda Ariya (1870-1949), who had long been a training partner of Kano, was a *nidan* in 1905. Honda was appointed instructor of the women's division of the Kodokan *Joshi-bu* and eventually obtained the rank of 8th *dan*.[37]

ADDING JUJUTSU AND AIKIDO

Apparently possessing boundless energy as well as growing doubts about *judo*, Sugino embarked on the study of classical *jujutsu* simultaneously with his training in *judo* and *Katori Shinto-ryu*. At the same time, he was running a *dojo* and operating his bone-setting practice. Moreover, at about the age of 20, Yoshino married a young woman with whom he had fallen in love.[38] Sadly, she died in childbirth, but apparently not before leaving him a son, Akio.*

In 1928, then a 4th *dan* in *judo*, Sugino began the study of one of the few remaining classical (*koryu*) styles of *jujutsu*—*Yoshin Koryu Jujutsu*—under a top instructor of the *Butokukai* named Kanaya Genro.[39] Sugino may well have met Kanaya through Kano's Kodokan out-reach program, as he did his *koryu kenjutsu* teachers. He trained in *Yoshin Koryu Jujutsu* for at least seven or eight years. In 1935, he assisted his instructor in a demonstration of his style at a large group performance for the Crown Prince at the Saineikan *dojo* on the grounds of the Imperial Palace. Among the other styles demonstrated were *Daito-ryu Aikijutsu*, led by a student of *Aikido* founder Ueshiba Morihei. Such demonstrations and contests in the presence of royalty were a regular occurrence from the 1920s through the mid-1940s.

Sugino apparently continued to train with Kanaya in *Yoshin Koryu Jujutsu* until at least the mid-1930s, reaching the rank of *kyoshi* (senior instructor). He frequently traveled around the country as a member of the newly established Society for the Promotion of Classical Japanese Martial Arts, headed by the minister of justice, himself a high-ranking *kyudo* (archery) master, putting on demonstrations of *jujutsu* and *Tenshin Shoden Katori Shinto-ryu* at various famous Shinto shrines. By this time, although he was apparently still teaching *judo*, he ceased competing and sought no higher rank in the art. "Kodokan *judo* had become a sport," he later recalled, "and I was not interested in that."[40]

---

* I was unable to find much information on Sugino's family. He remarried after his first wife's death and had four more sons (including the eldest, Shigeo, and his successor, Yukihiro) and two daughters. His younger sister, Sugino Kimiko was also highly trained in *Tenshin Shoden Katori Shinto-ryu*. He had another younger sister, Fusako, 20 years his junior.

YOSHIN KORYU JUJUTSU
楊心古流柔術

The history of "*Yoshin Koryu Jujutsu*" is convoluted and confusing. It was well known and influential in the early 20th century, but has since disappeared.[41] At first, there were several distinct "*Yoshin-ryu*" schools of *jujutsu*, but the one Sugino studied was the *Miura-ryu*, or *Miura Yoshin-ryu*, also known as *Yoshin Koryu*. The original style was created by Nakamura Sakyodayu Yoshikuni, who later took the name Miura Yoshin. It is said that his grandfather was Baba Mino no Kami Yorifusa, a retainer of the Koshu Takeda family. (It is remarkable how many schools of martial arts trace their origins to the pre-1600 fighting clan of the Takeda.) Being on the losing side when Toyotomi Hideyoshi unified Japan, the family changed its name from Nakamura to Miura, moved to the island of Shikoku, and opened a bone-setting clinic.

> Yoshikuni did further study in medicine and also expanded his study to include Chinese medicine, and even worked as an assistant to a Chinese doctor who operated a clinic in Bizen. Later he went to live in Miura village in Bizen no Kuni and changed his name to Miura Yoshin. Later he moved again, to Nagasaki, where he opened his own clinic. Under his father he had studied the jujutsu of the Daiin Ryu (or Taiin Ryu), which his grandfather is said to have founded. By combining his study of Daiin Ryu and his knowledge of Chinese medicine, Miura Yoshin is said to have developed his own unique jujutsu system.[42]

The history and lineage of the style has become lost, with only a few intermittent generations known. Abe Kanryu (1712-70) was apparently the sixth-generation head, followed by his nephew, Egami Tsukasa Umanosuke Taketsune (1747-95), who later took the name Kanryu to honor his teacher. Egami's successor, Totsuka Hikoemon Hidezumi (1772-1847), changed the name of the *ryuha* to *Egami-ryu* in honor of his teacher, but Totsuka's son and successor, Totsuka Hikosuke Hidetoshi, restored the name of the *ryuha* to *Yoshin-ryu*. The the ninth *soke* was Totsuka Hikosuke Hidetoshi (1812-86) who left the system to his son, tenth *soke*, Totsuka Hikokuro Hidemi (1842-1909).

However, another student who had received *menkyo kaiden* from the ninth *soke* was senior to Hidemi. His name was Imada Masayoshi. His chief disciple, Kanaya Motoyoshi (1843-1904), became *shihan* of the *Dai Nippon Butokukai*.[43]

Clearly, this Kanaya *Sensei* was not the man who taught Sugino; Kanaya died the year Sugino was born. Sugino's teacher likely was Kanaya's son (either natural or adopted).[44] According to Sugino, *Yoshin Koryu* was "more or less the same as the present Tenjin Shinyo-ryu or Kito-ryu Jujutsu."[45]

In fact, during the early days of Kano Jigoro's effort to establish his Kodokan *judo*, *Yoshin-ryu* was one of his chief rivals. In 1886, the Tokyo Metropolitan Police organized a *"shiai"* pitting fifteen of Kano's best against fifteen competitors from the *Totsuka-ha Yoshin-ryu* school—the most prestigious in Japan—supplemented by a handful of top students from other *jujutsu* schools.[46] The opposition was led by the Totsuka school of *Yoshin-ryu jujutsu*. In Kano's own words:

> Totsuka Hikosuke was considered the strongest *jujutsuka* of the Bakumatsu Period (end of the shogunate). After Hikosuke, (his son) Eimi carried the name of the school, and he trained many outstanding *jujutsuka*... In truth, Totsuka's side had powerful fighters and were no blowhards... When you mentioned the name Totsuka, you meant the greatest *jujutsu* masters of that era. My own *Tenshin Shinyo-ryu* and *Kito-ryu* (*jujutsu*) teachers were sorely pressed when they went up against Totsuka *jujutsu* masters at the shogunate's Komusho *dojo*...[47]

Complete records of the entire *shiai* appear no longer to exist, but recollections of a few highpoints remain. The first match pitted Tomita of Kodokan *Judo* against an unknown opponent. Tomita won his match, as did Yamashita Yoshikazu, apparently both with little struggle. Kano's student Yokoyama, however, faced the formidable Nakamura Hansuke of the *Ryoi Shinto-ryu* school. Yokoyama was 26 years old, and a bit over 5'6", weighing in at something over 200 pounds; Nakamura was 5'7" and also between 200-210 pounds. He was reputed to be one of the toughest men in Japan and could hang from a tree with a rope around his neck without feeling pain or passing out. It was to be a battle of the Titans, and their battle was indeed epic. It lasted just short of an hour before the referee—Master Hisatomi Tetsutaro of the prestigious *jujutsu* style of *Sekiguchi-ryu*—called it a draw. Hisatomi had to pry the contestants' fingers apart from each other because they had fought so long and hard their hands had cramped into claws.

Yokoyama walked off dejected, feeling he had let Kano and his Kodokan *Judo* down; in the eyes of the old *jujutsu* masters, a draw was as bad as a loss. But one more match remained: Saigo Shiro stepped forward to face Ukiji Entaro, the senior student of Tokutsa Eimi and the man who later became head master of the *Yoshin-ryu* style. Yokoyama's opponent had been big; Saigo's was huge. The 20-year-old Saigo, only 5'2" and about 128 pounds faced his much larger opponent in what looked to be a mismatch.

Saigo apparently started off rather lethargically, perhaps intimidated by the size of his opponent. Entaro quickly grasped Saigo's *gi* and executed a powerful throw. Saigo rose high into the air as the crowd gasped. The Kodokan players must have winced, or closed their eyes, waiting for the loud thud of Saigo hitting the mat and losing the last fight of the contest. But the thud never happened. Somehow the athletic Saigo spun in the air—some accounts said he did a somersault—and landed on his forearm and knees. Some accounts indicate that Entaro continuously attacked Saigo for 10 minutes or more with one attempted throw after another. Each time, Saigo's balance and athleticism allowed him to escape being decisively thrown.

Finally, angry at being nearly defeated, Saigo rose with fire in his eyes, grabbed Entaro and pulled him off balance, then threw him with his own specialty, *yama arashi* or "mountain storm." It was Saigo's secret technique and no one today knows exactly what it was. Some have speculated that it was a cross between *seioinage* and *hanegoshi*; others opine that *yama arashi* was simply Saigo's fiery style of attacking like a mountain storm.

In any event, Entaro took a hard fall. Momentarily stunned, he slowly began to rise, angry and confused. On the sidelines, Yokoyama is said to have whispered, "No one gets up from Saigo's *yama arashi* that fast. This Entaro is one tough guy." Yamashita, who had already won his bout, shouted out, "Watch our, Saigo, watch out!"

But before Entaro could get his bearings, Saigo jumped on him, slamming him to the ground, apparently with an *osotogari*. This time, Entaro didn't get up. He was out with a concussion. The referee declared Saigo the victor.

The Kodokan—a new organization run by a *jujutsu* instructor who had only really had five years of training in two different styles—had just decisively proved its superiority over the best of the traditional *jujutsu* schools. Accounts differ, and may confuse several similar *shiai*, but Kodokan *Judo* had won either nine of ten matches, with one draw, or 12 of 15, with one draw and two losses.[48]

Although the style of *Yoshin Koryu* itself apparently has died out, some of its techniques undoubtedly live on in *judo*; Kano put together his Kodokan *judo* in part based on *Kito-ryu jujutsu* and probably invited teachers of *Yoshin-ryu* to teach seniors at the Kodokan. Moreover, elements of *Yoshin Koryu* almost certainly were incorporated by Sugino into his teachings. Finally, *Wado-ryu* (和道流) *karate* of Ohtsuka Hironori and the *Shindo Jinen-ryu* (神道自然流) of Konishi Yasuhiro probably also contain echoes of *Yoshin-ryu*.

Konishi with Mabuni Kenwa

Ohtsuka practicing *jujutsu* with his son, Jiro.

In the midst of this searching for answers to the *gokui* (secrets) of *budo*, Sugino also began about 1935 to study *Aikido*. Ueshiba was already a well-established figure in the martial arts community, and a person who had attracted favorable attention from Kano Jigoro himself. In fact, Sugino would have been familiar with the famous story of Kano's visit to Ueshiba's *dojo* some years earlier. Kano had taken several of his best students, including later-10th *dan*s Nagaoka Shuichi (1876-1952) and Mifune Kyuzo (1883-1965), each of whom was considered a *"judo* genius."

> Kano *Sensei*, along with two or three others including Mr. Mifune, an instructor of the Kodokan, and Mr. Nagaoka went to Ueshiba *Sensei*'s *dojo* in Shinjuku to observe his training. It is said that Kano *Sensei* remarked after seeing the training: "This is true *Judo*." Mr. Nagaoka then is supposed to have made a joke saying, "*Sensei*, then is what we are doing false *judo*?" Kano *Sensei* meant it in the broader sense. He praised *aikido* explaining that it was not just *judo* but *judo* in a wider sense... Kano *Sensei* asked Ueshiba *Sensei* to teach this art to some of his *deshi*.[49]

In another version of the story, Nagaoka's response was more pointed: "Watching the training, Kano is said to have remarked in admiration, 'Now that is true *judo*!' Nagaoka was apparently taken aback and upset by this unexpected comment and challenged his teacher by asking impulsively: 'Then the *judo* we are practicing is not real? Is what we do at the Kodokan nothing but a lie?' Kano explained that he had not intended to imply such a thing and that he had simply meant that *aikido* was *judo* in a broad sense. He continued to praise Ueshiba and later asked him to teach some of his own students."[50]

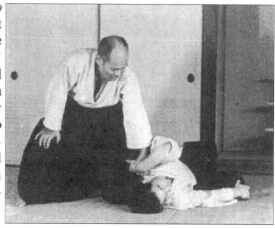

Ueshiba Morihei

Sugino had been acquainted with Ueshiba since the early 1930s. He later recalled "that upon their first meeting he was surprised to find before his eyes a smallish yet extremely robust man with a broad smile spanning his face. He wondered if this could really be the Ueshiba he had heard so much about."⁵¹ Watching him perform, the *judo* 4ᵗʰ *dan* and competitive champion was impressed by Ueshiba's casualness and unpretentious manner.

> He watched Ueshiba's movements intently, noting how his body seemed to be the personification of pure energy as he shifted airily about the room tossing his attackers this way and that, with the occasional pin thrown in for good measure. Back then, those lacking a deeper understanding of *bujutsu* tended to be deceived by the beauty and superb skill of Ueshiba's *aikido* demonstrations, and would often assume they were merely prearranged. But Sugino had reached a point in his training where he was capable of easily distinguishing real martial technique from fake choreography, and he knew he was seeing the genuine article.

> On this point he says: "If it isn't so good that it makes people think it's fake, then it's not true *aikido*. Ueshiba's techniques were truly alive, whether he was empty-handed or holding a staff or sword. You could almost 'see' the *ki* flowing from his hands." He continues: "People like [former high-ranking *sumo* wrestler] Tenryu probably inwardly thought that Ueshiba *Sensei*'s techniques looked fake when they first saw them. But Ueshiba *Sensei* saw right through such doubts. To Tenryu he said, "Ah, Tenryu, you're so very strong" and slid his hand up to pat Tenryu on the shoulder. But with this simple, subtle movement he unbalanced the wrestler completely. Impressed by Ueshiba's demonstration, Sugino enrolled in the *dojo* immediately.⁵²

This enrolment apparently was in 1931 or 1932. Sugino took to *aikido* with the same enthusiasm and natural talent with which he had early embraced *judo*.* Although Ueshiba taught in the old style, demonstrating techniques once or twice but almost never explaining or providing detailed instruction, Sugino's *judo* practice gave him a leg up in seeing what Ueshiba was doing, and he progressed very rapidly. By 1935—after only three or four years of training—Ueshiba awarded Sugino a teaching license, and after the War, Sugino opened only the second *aikido dojo*—aside from Ueshiba's *honbu*—in Japan. Ueshiba's son and successor, Kishomaru, would visit periodically to teach and update Sugino on the latest developments from headquarters.⁵⁴

---

* Interestingly, Sugino said he was introduced to Ueshiba by "Konishi *Sensei*." This very likely was Konishi Yasuhiro (小西康裕, 1893-1983), who had studied both *Muso-ryu* and *Takenouchi-ryu jujutsu*, and *kendo*. He later (continued)

Ueshiba during this period seemed to be searching for a true successor—Kishomaru, Ueshiba's third son, had taken a fulltime job with a securities firm and did not appear to plan to teach *aikido* for a living.[55] He had a number of highly accomplished students, including Tomiki Kenji (富木 謙治,1900-1979), Mochizuku Minoru (望月 稔, 1907-2003) and Shioda Gozo (塩田 剛三, 1915-1994) but Ueshiba seems to have staked his future on a young *kendo* expert named Nakakura Kiyoshi (中倉清, 1910-2000) a student of the famed Nakayama Hakudo (中山 博道, 1872-1958), Maruta Kanehiro, Haga Junichi (羽賀準一), and others. Nakakura married Ueshiba's daughter in 1932 at the age of 22 and was taken into the Ueshiba home as an adopted son and *uchi deshi* (training disciple) of Ueshiba. Nakakura later remembered, however, that

> Although I was practicing *aikido*, I found Mr. Ueshiba to be superhuman, and felt that I would never be able to master the techniques he was doing, and therefore could not succeed him. I felt that I should not cling to the position as his successor. Then I went to see Nakayama [Hakudo] *Sensei*, and told him that I did think I would be able to succeed Ueshiba, and would like to leave the Ueshiba family. *Sensei* said that he understood, but told me to wait until he had talked to Mr. Ueshiba. That was just before I left the Kobukan [Ueshiba's *dojo*] in 1937.[56]

Ueshiba seems next to have looked to Sugino as a possible successor, reportedly asking him to "consider devoting himself professionally to *aikido*," but Sugino, with a growing family and financial responsibilities, declined.[57] Nonetheless, Sugino continued to teach *aikido* along with *judo* and *Tenshin Shoden Katori Shinto-ryu* for the rest of his life.

---

studied under Ueshiba for a time. Konishi was instrumental in helping Funakoshi Gichin become established at Keio University, and he studied Okinawan *karate* under Funakoshi, Mabuni Kenwa, Motobu Choki, and Miyagi Chojun. He later became a fulltime martial arts instructor, establishing the *Ryobukan* ("House of Martial Arts Excellence"), where he taught *karate, kendo,* and *jujutsu*. He was one of the most influential Japanese martial artists of his era.[53]

TAKING UP THE SWORD

mong the masters Kano invited to the Kodokan were four senior experts of *Tenshin Shoden Katori Shinto-ryu Bujutsu,* probably the oldest extant martial system in Japan and one of the most highly respected.

Considered one of the fountainheads of Japanese martial tradition, *Katori Shinto-ryu* had never been taught outside the Chiba region. Kano, however, asked whether some arrangement could be made to have the style taught in Tokyo as well. This caused a great stir within the school and it was discussed at length whether or not the request should be accommodated. Eventually it was decided that, as the tradition was in danger of falling into obscurity, it should be actively disseminated in Tokyo to prevent this.

The school dispatched four *shihan*: Narimichi Tamai, Sozaemon Kuboki, Tanekichi Ito, and Ichizo Shiinato [Shiina] to teach the style at the Kodokan. It was arranged that these four should also stop in Kawasaki on their way home, training with Sugino there on Sunday afternoons and Monday mornings.[58]

Despite his previous unsatisfying experience with *kendo*, Sugino took to *Katori Shinto-ryu* immediately. Perhaps it was the difference between wielding a *shinai* and working with a real sword, but Sugino immersed himself in the complex curriculum of this ancient style. *Katori Shinto-ryu kata* tend to be more combative, long and intricate, and dynamic than the *kata* developed for *kendo* students, with *uchidachi* and *shidachi* attacking back and forth in lengthy exchanges, using diverse techniques and identifying and attacking openings in the opponent's defenses.[59]

Sugino not only fell in love with the sword aspect of *Katori Shinto-ryu*, but began to delve deeply into the style's huge curriculum, which includes *bo, naginata, yari, shuriken* and *ryoto* (two-sword) techniques. He spent two years training under Tamai and Ito, then 10 years as a disciple of Shiina.[60]

Although *Tenshin Shoden Katori Shinto-ryu* was to become Sugino's major preoccupation—and occupation—his training was interrupted by forays into new employment and he was not yet finished expanding his martial experience and expertise.

TENSHIN SHODEN KATORI SHINTO-RYU
天眞正傳香取神道流

Tenshin Shoden Katori Shinto-ryu is widely considered to be the oldest continuous martial arts system in Japan, tracing its origins back to between 1447-1480.[61] Its founder was Iizasa Choisai Ienao (飯篠長威斎家直, 1387-1488), the son of a *goshi* (farmer-*samurai*) in the service of the Chiba family in Iizasa village (from which the family took its surname), Chiba prefecture, and of the Askikaga *shogun*, Yoshimasa 足利 義政, 1436–1490). From a very early age, Ienao showed great talent with the spear, sword, and *naginata*, and reportedly participated in a number of battles in which he was never personally defeated. Like all *samurai* of that period, he trained in comprehensive martial arts as taught by the elders and instructors of his clan. This included virtually all weapons (archery, sword, spear, *naginata*, short sword, staff, two-sword technique, throwing darts, etc.) as well as strategy, fortification, intelligence collection, campaign logistics, etc.

Iizasa Choisai Ienao

At some point when Ienao was about 60 years old, the *daimyo* (feudal lord) to whom he was attached was deposed, throwing the Chiba clan and the Iizasa family out of work. Ienao took advantage of this opportunity to retire from his family (his children were almost certainly grown up, but his wife's status is unclear) and other responsibilities. He moved to the vicinity of the famous Katori Shrine (see below) to devote himself to religious purification and intense training. Ienao must have been relatively wealthy when he undertook this retreat: he reportedly donated 1,000 *koku* of rice—traditionally, one *koku*, about 300 pounds, was enough to sustain a person for a year—to the Shrine and another 1,000 *koku* to build a Buddhist temple, the *Shintokusan Shimpuku-ji* at Miyamoto village, Otsuki, Yamanashi prefecture.[62]

Ienao apparently had taken at least one servant with him because, according to legend, one day that servant was washing one of Ienao's favorite horses, using the water from a sacred spring near the shrine. Shortly thereafter, the horse mysteriously sickened and died, leading Ienao to reflect on the enormous power of the Katori Shrine's resident Shinto deity, Futsunushi-no-mikoto. (See below.)

As a result of this incident, Ienao took on the religious name of "Choisai" and decide to engage in 1,000 days of austere training. Although already 60 years of age, Choisai rose every day at 1:30 am to pray at the shrine and undergo Shinto purification rites. At 2:30, he returned to his quarters and recited Buddhist scriptures. Later in the morning, he went back to the shrine for additional worship before beginning a full day of arduous martial training.[63]

One day while engaging in hard training—one account says he was repeatedly striking a plum tree with his *bokken*—the god Futsunushi-no mikoto appeared to him in the form of a young boy sitting in the tree. The boy handed Choisai a volume on the martial arts called *Heiho Shinsho* (it was to be the first of many volumes, with Choisai writing the sequels) and told him "You shall be a great teacher of all the swordsmen under the sun."[64]

Choisai's skill level is attested to in an almost certainly apocryphal story. According to a legend passed down in the style:

> when the founder was challenged by another swordsman that came to his house, he would greet him courteously. Next he would spread a mat on some *kumazasa*[,] that is dwarf bamboo or bamboo grass, and sit down on top of it without as much as bending its stalks. Then he would invite the challenger to sit next to him. It is said that after seeing this feat any challenger would back down. This is known as "*kumazasa no taiza*" or "*kumazasa no oshie*" and can respectively by translated as "showdown/face off of the dwarf bamboo" or "teaching of the dwarf bamboo".[65]

Although Choisai never fought another battle or duel, and in fact became an advocate of peace, he became instructor to numerous martial artists, and his style became the ancestor of dozens of later *ryuha* of swordsmanship and other martial arts. He is said to have named his new style *Tenshin Shoden Katori Shinto-ryu* ("Heavenly Martial Tradition Transmitted by the Gods in the Katori Jingu" or Shrine). Over the years, the name has been changed a number of times:

> At the time of the third headmaster Iizasa Wakasa no Kami Morinobu the tradition was known as *Shinryo Shinto Ryu* (神慮神道流), under the 15th head Iizasa Shurinosuke Moriteru as *Shinto Ryu* (新刀流). In other domains the tradition was also often referred to as Katori Shinto Ryu (香取神道流). Around the Bakumatsu period (end of the shogun era) the school was called Katori Shinto Ryu (香取神刀流). Under the nineteenth head, Iizasa Shurinosuke Kinjiro [in 1940] the school was renamed *Tenshin Shoden Katori Shintoryu* (天眞正傳香取神道流), and has been known as such until the present time.[66]

Tenshin Shoden Katori Shinto-ryu claims to have had a continuous and direct descent of *soke* (family heads) since Choisai. This seems unlikely, however. Although some sources report that the second headmaster, Wakasa-no-kami Morichika, was the eldest son of Choisai, that seems hard to imagine given that Choisai died at the age of 102.[67] His eldest son would likely have been 80 or older, something quite rare in those days. Moreover, it would be unusual for a family to survive 20 generations with a son in each generation to inherit the position of *soke*. It seems likely that, as with many Japanese families of the time, at least some of the successors were adopted (either students who were adopted or by marriage to a daughter of the Iizasa family.) As will be seen below, it is known that there was no successor to the 18th *soke*, and it was another 11 years before a marriage produced the 19th *soke*.

Tenshin Shoden Katori Shinto-ryu is different from many other Japanese martial arts—even fellow *koryu* (ancient styles) in several ways:
- After some 500 years, the style remains a comprehensive *heiho* (martial way) including a huge and complicated curriculum. The Iizasa family, which has headed the style since its formation, is in possession of a large number of "secret" scrolls which are shown only to a few of the very highest masters and family members.

- The style has never been sponsored or controlled by any outside source, such as a *daimyo* or financial backer. It has remained completely independent for some 500 years.
- Esoteric knowledge and practice are integral to the style. Its study of *chikujojutsu* (construction of fortifications), for example, follows the teachings of *gogyo* (esoteric mysteries and practices) and Taoist concepts; students are indoctrinated in *inyo kigaku*, comprising Buddhist esoteric teachings or *mikkyo*, *Kuji kiri*, (nine symbolic hand postures or *mudras*), astrology, and divination. Otake Risuke's three volume book on the style (especially Volume 2, pages 26-34, and Volume 3, pages 12-21) explain and demonstrate some of this esoteric practice.
- Entrants are required to execute a *keppan*, a sworn oath signed and sealed in the entrant's own blood to abide by the policies of the *ryu*, including not teaching or showing its teachings to outsiders, not engaging in fights, avoiding gambling and dissolute living, etc.
- In April 1960 *Katori Shinto ryu Heiho* was recognized as a part of the cultural heritage of Japan—the first Japanese martial art so honored.

Iizasa Choisai Ienao's grave.

TENSHIN SHODEN KATORI SHINTO-RYU LINEAGE

Founder: Iizasa Choisai Ienao (Iga-no-kami)
2nd headmaster: Iizasa Wakasa-no-kami Morichika
3rd headmaster: Iizasa Wakasa-no-kami Morinobu
4th headmaster: Iizasa Yamashiro-no-kami Moritsuna
5th headmaster: Iizasa Saemon-no-jo Morihide
6th headmaster: Iizasa Oi-no-kami Morishige
7th headmaster: Iizasa Shuri-no-suke Morinobu
8th headmaster: Iizasa Shuri-no-suke Morinaga
9th headmaster: Iizasa Shuri-no-suke Morihisa
10th headmaster: Iizasa Shuri-no-suke Morisada
11th headmaster: Iizasa Shuri-no-suke Morishige
12th headmaster: Iizasa Shuri-no-suke Moritsugu
13th headmaster: Iizasa Shuri-no-suke Morikiyo
14th headmaster: Iizasa Shuri-no-suke Nagateru
15th headmaster: Iizasa Shuri-no-suke Moriteru
16th headmaster: Iizasa Shuri-no-suke Morishige (Kanrokusai)
17th headmaster: Iizasa Shuri-no-suke Morifusa
18th headmaster: Iizasa Shuri-no-suke Morisada (1839-1898)
19th headmaster: Iizasa Shuri-no-suke Kinjiro
20th headmaster: Iizasa Shuri-no-suke Yasusada (飯篠 修理亮 快貞, current head of the family)[68]

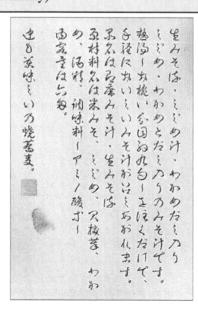

Example of *keppan* (blood oath) Source: http://www.jitakyoeibudo.it/index.php?dir=pagine&id=41&m=y&pid=1,92,93.

KATORI SHRINE

The Katori Shrine is located in the city of Katori in Chiba Prefecture. It was built for the Shinto deity Futsunushi-no-mikoto or Futsunushi-no-kami (経津主神). Near by in Kashima, Ibaragi Prefecture is the Kashima Shrine, which was dedicated to the deity of the sword, Takemikazuchi-no-kami. Only three shrines—Kashima, Katori, and the great shrine at Ise—are allowed to use the title "shrine" (*jingu*). The Katori *jingu* is the head shrine of the approximately 400 Katori subsidiary shrines around the country (located primarily in the Kanto region of eastern Japan). It is believed that the Katori Shrine was first built in the 18th year of the reign of the emperor Jimmu Tenno (642 BC) to honor Futsunushi-no-mikoto, the patron of national security, industrial development and material values. Katori Shrine was traditionally reconstructed every 20 years, until the system fell apart during the Warring States period. The current structure was built in 1700 and is designated an Important Cultural Property. The Romon gate of Katori Shrine was also constructed in 1700 and is also designated an Important Cultural Property. It displays the shrine's name plaque written by Fleet Admiral Togo Heihachiro, the hero of the Russo-Japanese War. For centuries the Katori Shrine has been the destination for pilgrimages by martial artists seeking divine inspiration and assistance to progress in the martial arts. An altar to the gods of the Kashima and Katori shrines can be found in many traditional *dojo* in Japan, including the headquarters of the *Tenshin Shoden Katori Shinto-ryu*.[69]

FUTSUNUSHI-NO-MIKOTO

The deity Futsunushi-no-mikoto plays an important role in Japanese mythology. The deity of fire and lightning, he became a god of war and a general for the sun deity Amaterasu-o-mi-kami, the ancestor of the Japanese emperors. Futsunushi assisted Amaterasu by pacifying the country to cement the rule of Ninigi-no-mikoto, Amaterasu's grandson. As a result, Futsunushi became a tutelary *kami* of swords, interpreted by some as the divine personification of the sacred sword Futsu-no-mitama, and revered as one of the ancestral *kami* (*sojin*) of the Fujiwara clan. Futsunushi's activities frequently overlap with those of the *kami* Takemikazuchi, such as when the latter joins the former in descending from heaven to pacify the Central Land of Reed Plains (Ashihara no Nakatsukuni). It is believed that Futsunushi was a martial tutelary of the warrior Mononobe clan, one of Japan's earliest and most powerful clans, but with the rise of the Nakatomi clan, his divine attributes were gradually appropriated by Takemikazuchi. Futsunushi is the central *kami* (*saijin*) at Katori Jingu and other shrines.[70]

CONNECTIONS AND DESCENDANT SCHOOLS

According to legend, a number of the most famous and successful swordsmen in Japanese history trained with Iizasa Choisai Ienao or his successors; many later created their own famous *ryuha* (styles). Among them were Kamiizumi-Ise-no-kami Nobutsuna (上泉伊勢守藤原信綱,1508-1577), founder of *Shinkage-ryu*; Matsumoto Bizen-no-kami Masanobu (松本備前守尚勝, 1467-1524), one of the three founders of *Kashima Shin-ryu*; Tsukahara Tosa-no-kami (塚原土佐守安幹), who instructed Tsukahara Bokuden Takamoto (塚原卜伝高幹,1489-1571), who is credited with founding the *Kashima Shinto-ryu*. Others included Kushibuchi Magobei of *Shindo Isshin-ryu*; Iba Zesuiken of *Shingyoto-ryu*; Okada Soemon of *Ryogo-ryu*; and Idori Kyoun Tamenobu of *Ko-ryu*.

One interesting sidelight concerns the famous Miyamoto Musashi (宮本 武蔵, c. 1584–1645), whose name appears in a medieval visitor list to the style's *dojo*. Musashi had defeated a young and arrogant but very skilled Muso Gonnosuke Katsukichi (夢想權之助勝吉) sometime between 1596-1614, but had declined to seriously injure or kill him. Deeply frustrated by his loss, Gonnosuke undertook a lengthy period of *shugyo* (austere training), much like that of Iizasa, then apparently set off on a *musha shugyo* (traveling around challenging other schools and fighters). After one especially exhausting training sessions, he collapsed from fatigue and reputedly had a vision of a divine being in the form of a child, telling him cryptically: "Know the solar plexus [of your opponent] with a round stick". (In another version he had the vision in a dream late at night.)

As a result, he created a *jo* longer than the average *katana* of the day, about 128 cm as opposed to the sword's total length of approximately 100 cm, and set out to use that length to his advantage in a fight. In a rematch with Musashi, Gonnosuke allegedly came out on top, using the superior length of the *jo* to keep Musashi's swords out of range and thus hindering him from using his X-shaped two-sword technique effectively. Gonnosuke had Musashi at his mercy but let him live as a way of returning the favor granted in the first duel.* It is alleged that Gonnosuke had trained in *Tenshin Shoden Katori Shinto-ryu* and that the style helped him create his own *Shindo Muso-ryu*.

---

* The claim that Musashi was ever defeated by Gonnosuke is still a matter of debate and is generally treated very skeptically. Another version of the story says that Musashi and Gonnosuke fought to a deadlock, and the match ended in a draw, as no one could move without leaving an opening.

DESCENDANT SCHOOLS

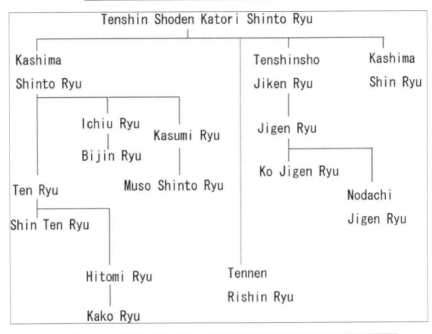

Katori Jingu

Chart source: http://wiki.samurai-archives.com/index.php?title=Tenshin_Shoden_Katori_Shinto_ryu. For a much more detailed lineage of related styles (in Japanese), see *Nihon no Kenjutsu*. Tokyo: Gakken, 2013, page 143.

TENSHIN SHODEN KATORI SHINTO-RYU CURRICULUM

I. Sword techniques - 剣術 (*Tachi Jutsu*, Standing techniques)

    1. Basics of the Sword, 表之太刀, (*Omote no Tachi*)

        A. *Itsutsu no tachi.* (First *bokken kata*)
        B. *Nanatsu no tachi.* (Second *bokken kata*)
        C. *Kasumi no tachi.* (Third *bokken kata*)
        D. *Hakka no tachi.* (Fourth *bokken kata*)

    2. Five Teachings of the Sword, 五教之太刀, (*Gogyo no Tachi*)

        A. *Mitsu no tachi.* (First *bokken kata*)
        B. *Yotsu no tachi.* (Second *bokken kata*)
        C. *In no tachi.* (Third *bokken kata*)
        D. *Sha no tachi.* (Fourth *bokken kata*)
        E. *Hotsu no tachi.* (Fifth *bokken kata*)

    3. Two swords techniques, 両刀術, (*Ryotojutsu*)

        A. *Eigetsu no tachi.* (First two-sword *kata*)
        B. *Suigetsu no tachi.* (Second two-sword *kata*)
        C. *Isonami no tachi.* (Third two-sword *kata*)
        D. *Murakumo no tachi.* (Fourth two-sword *kata*)

    4. Short sword *kata*, 小太刀術, (*Gokui no Kodachi*)

        A. *Hangetsu no kodachi.* (First short sword *kata*)
        B. *Suigetsu no kodachi.* (Second short sword *kata*)
        C. *Seigan no kodachi.* (Third short sword *kata*)

    5. Sword drawing and cutting from a sitting position, 居合 (*Iai*)

        A. *Kusa nagi no ken.*
        B. *Nuki tsuke no ken.*
        C. *Nuki uchi no ken.*
        D. *Uken.*
        E. *Saken.*
        F. *Happo ken.*

    6. Sword drawing and cutting from a standing position, 立合抜刀術, (*Tachi-ai Batto jutsu*)

        A. *Yuki ai gyaku nuki no tachi.*
        B. *Zengo Chidori no tachi.*

C. *Yuki ai Migi Chidori no tachi.*
D. *Gyakku nuki no tachi.*
E. *Nuki uchi no tachi.*

7. Long staff techniques, 棒術, (*Bojutsu*)

   A. *Seri ai no bo.*
   B. *Sune hishigi no bo.*
   C. *Sayu no bo.*
   D. *Kazahazushi no bo.*
   E. *Hana tsurube no bo.*
   F. *Tate nami no bo.*

8. Glaive (curved spear) techniques, 長刀術, (*Naginatajutsu*)

   A. *Itsutsu no naginata.*
   B. *Nanatsu no naginata.*
   C. *Kasumi no naginata.*
   D. *Hakka no naginata.*

9. Spear techniques, 表之槍, (*Omote no yari*)

   A. *Hiryu no yari.*
   B. *Koryu no yari.*
   C. *Tsuki dome no yari.*
   D. *Anya no yari.*
   E. *Denko no vari.*
   F. *Yoru no va vari.*

10. Weapon throwing techniques. 手裏剣術,(Spike throwing; *Shurikenjutsu*)

The *Gogyo* and *Gokui kata* are only taught to advanced practitioners after many years of fundamental practice.

Other, more advanced areas of study of the school include:

- *Yawara-jutsu* (Grappling and knife fighting)
- *Ninjutsu* (Intelligence gathering and analysis)
- *Chikujojutsu* (Field fortification art)
- *Gunbai-Heiho* (Strategy and tactics)
- *Ten/Don Chirigaku* (Astronomy & geomantic divination)
- *In-Yo kigaku* (Philosophical and mystical aspects derived from esoteric Buddhism).[71]

KATORI SHINTO-RYU KENJUTSU MASTERS

Iizasa Shuri-no-suke Yasusada
飯篠修理亮快貞

Sugino Yoshio
杉野嘉男

Otake Minamoto no Takeyuki Risuke (大竹源健之利典, born March 10, 1926).

Sugino Yukihiro
(杉野至寛, born 1937)

TEACHING AND HEALING DURING THE WAR

Sugino must have led a frenetic life during the 1930s, between teaching *judo* and *kenjutsu* and continuing to study *kenjutsu, jujutsu,* and *aikido,* and trying to raise a family. In 1935, when "the *koryu budo* organization, *Nihon Kobudo Shinkokai* [Japan Federation for the Preservation of Ancient Martial Arts] was founded, *Katori Shinto-ryu* was represented by Tamai and Shiina *sensei*, together with Sugino."[72] By 1937, Sugino held the position of "Instructor of *Budo*" at Chiba Teachers' College and taught *Katori Shinto-ryu* in various places in Chiba prefecture, as well at Fuji Elementary School in Asakusa. He also taught *naginata* at Yokohama Girls' Vocational School and *judo* at Keio Secondary School and, from 1939, at Keio University, where he had first started learning the art.[73]

A relatively young Sugino throwing *shuriken*, part of the style's curriculum.

Somehow, despite top scores on the conscription examination, Sugino was not called up for active duty, nor do available documents indicate he taught for the military—as many *budo* teachers did. He reportedly had a nominal position as an "auxiliary transport soldier," a low-level position with no prestige.[74] Sugino later attributed his lack of military service duty to "sheer dumb luck: 'I passed the eligibility exam with flying colors, but fortunately my number in the lottery just never came up.' Whatever behind-the-scenes reasons there may have been for his exemption will never be known, but in any case he says he is glad to have been able to pass the war years without having to kill a single soul."[75]

In addition to his teaching duties, Sugino trained weekly until the end of the war at the *hombu dojo* in Chiba founded by Iizasa Shuri-no-suke Morisada, where he also instructed the younger generation.[76] (For the rather confused situation at the *hombu dojo*, see below.)

As the War situation deteriorated, Sugino went from blacking out his home and *dojo* against U.S. night-time air raids to being burned out. His home city of

Kawasaki became a sea of flames as American bombers continued their forays over the island. As the conflagration made its way toward his home and *dojo*, Sugino rushed outside, clutching to his breast a great bundle of *yari* (spears) and *naginata* that he was determined to save. He took his family to the countryside of Fukushima to stay with the family of one of his students, who had invited them to seek shelter there. "The trains were jammed to capacity and beyond with people fleeing the city," he remembers. "All the way to Fukushima people were frowning and giving us dirty looks whenever I tried to squeeze into a train carriage with that awkward bundle of long weapons."

Once in Fukushima, Sugino spent most of his time training or caring for the injured and gradually the family settled in. In fact, they even began to find Fukushima rather agreeable and were considering staying there. Then came the end of the war. Sugino was at Anahara hot springs when he heard the emperor's broadcast announcing Japan's unconditional surrender. He recalls feeling completely stunned, drained of all will and energy, as if everything he knew had suddenly been annulled. But he knew it would be best to return to Kawasaki and rebuild life there. As it happened, he was just in the process of treating an elderly man who had broken his arm, so he sent his family on ahead of him and stayed a while longer until the treatment was finished. Fortunately a certain individual was able to assist the Sugino family in securing a new place to live and start anew. Still, most of the men in the country had not yet returned from the war and for a while there was no way to even think about resuming training at the Sugino *dojo* as it had been before.[77]

The Sugino family faced its share of hardships, having to start its own vegetable garden and buy rice on the black market—and Yoshio sacrificed even more to make sure his elderly father got enough to eat—but Yoshio's profession as a bone setter meant his business was very busy treating both those injured by the U.S. attacks on the home islands and many injured returning soldiers.[78]

In addition, the Occupation headquarters quickly banned the teaching of practice of all martial arts, associating them with the militarist trends that had fostered Japan's aggression. Sugino dutifully turned over two swords to the Occupation authorities as they demanded—he never saw them again—but, of course, continued his own training behind closed doors.[79] By 1949-50, the ban was slowly being eased, especially on *judo*, archery, and a modified system of *kendo*,[80] and in 1950 Sugino built a new *dojo*. He "arranged for some of his students to take over the bone-setting clinic so that he could devote himself exclusively to *budo*. Friends said he had become more rounded (perhaps mellowed by the hardships of the war and postwar years) but his enthusiasm for the martial arts remained unchecked."[81]

Sugino practicing *iai*.

SUGINO: BEHIND-THE-SCENES MOVIE STAR

Sugino Yoshio began his collaboration with the movie industry in 1937 when he served as a technical advisor on the use of the *yari* (spear) in a movie on Ogai Mori (森 鷗外, 1862-1922), a Japanese surgeon general, poet, novelist, and translator (from German, Dutch and Chinese).[82] He subsequently worked as a consultant on a number of theatrical and cinematic projects. But it was the early 1950s that he became most famous—at least among the *cognoscenti*—when Japan's premier movie director, Kurosawa Akira, called on Sugino to help choreograph a new movie on a *samurai* story. Always the innovator, Kurosawa wanted to get away from the *chambara* (fake and flashy) style of swordplay in the movies and present martial combat as it would actually have been experienced by the pre-Edo and early Edo period warriors.

> Kurosawa had already made a number of films including *Drunken Angel, Rashomon*, and *To Live* that were regarded as masterpieces. His next project was to be a *samurai* drama in which the stiff martial arts choreography typically used in such films would be replaced by something closer to the real thing. He had contacted the Ministry of Education for an introduction to a suitable instructor. The Ministry relayed the request to the Society for the Promotion of Classical Japanese Martial Arts who suggested Yoshio Sugino of the *Katori Shinto-ryu* and Junzo Sasamori of the *Ono-ha Itto-ryu*.[83]

Sasamori was well known as one of the finest swordsmen of his age and a major figure in the popularization of the new competitive *kendo* as well as the *koryu* on Ono-ha Itto-ryu. Born in 1886, Sasamori *Hanshi* was Sugino's senior by a considerable amount, and it was an honor to be asked to work with him.

In May 1953, Kurosawa pulled together Sugino, Sasamori, and the principal actors, including Toshiro Mifune, at an upscale restaurant to explain his concept.

Sasamori Junzo (笹森 順造, 1886-1976)

The movie was to be the classic, *Seven Samurai*. Mifune was already a well-established actor who had engaged in considerable on-screen swordplay, for example in the movie *Roshomon*. But Kurosawa asked the two experts "What should a sword fight really look like on film?"

Sugino was delighted to be able to participate in presenting real swordsmanship to the public. Due to other commitments, Sasamori soon pulled out, leaving Sugino as the sole choreographer.

> Assisted by his student Sumie Ishibashi [a woman student and distant relative], he demonstrated the sword and *iai* of *Katori Shinto-ryu* in a way that gave both Kurosawa and his cast a strong sense of what *bujutsu* was really about. Something that caught Kurosawa's attention was Sugino's solid, well-balanced personal demeanour, and he ordered the actors to emulate this as best they could including the way he walked, the way he kneeled down and any other aspects of his everyday manner they might notice. Kurosawa saw that there was a significant difference in stability between ordinary people and the samurai of old who spent their days with heavy swords at their waists.[84]

Mifune (left), Sugino (center), Kurosawa (right, in hat and glasses).

The result, of course, was a film classic that not only drew worldwide attention to Kurosawa and Mifune, but was copied by Hollywood in the famous 1960 Western, *The Magnificent Seven* starring Yul Brynner, Eli Wallach, Steve McQueen, Charles Bronson, and James Coburn.

Sugino would go on to collaborate with Kurosawa and Mifune on several more films, including *Duel at Ichioji Temple* (1955), *The Hidden Fortress* (1958), and *Yojimbo* (1961). He also worked on such films as *Yagyu Bugeicho* (1958, directed by Inagaki Hiroshi and starring Mifune and others), *Musashi* (1954), and *Duel at Ganryu Island* (1956, both also directed by Inagaki Hiroshi and starring Toshiro Mifune as Musashi Miyamoto and Koji Tsuruta as Kojiro Sasaki.)

Mifune (left) and Sugino (right).

DECADES OF DEDICATION

Sugino Yoshio continued to teach his *Tenshin Shoden Katori Shinto-ryu* in his Kawasaki *dojo* for nearly 50 years after the end of the War. The main line of the style remained relatively secret until the American martial artist and former Marine officer and veteran of the Pacific War against the Japanese, Donn Draeger, was accepted as a student and began to expose the public to the ancient art. Sugino *Sensei*, however, was more open almost from the beginning, permitting foreigners to train, both on a short– and long-term basis. Although Sugino appears to have given up *judo* altogether once he retired to teaching at just his *dojo*, his training retained a strong element of *aikido*, and Sugino and his school kept up close ties with both the *Tenshin Shoden Katori Shinto-ryu hombu dojo* and Ueshiba's *Aikikai*. In fact, Sugino was often invited to put on demonstrations at *aikido* gatherings, and he was a regular participant in the frequent *embu* (demonstrations, sometimes accompanied by *kata* competitions among *koryu budo*).

In 1966, the *Dai Nippon Butokukai* awarded the degree of *hanshi* to Sugino Yoshio. In 1982, International Martial Arts Federation (IMAF or *Kokusai Budoin*, 国際武道院) granted him the 10th *dan* and the title of *meijin* ("brilliant man" or martial arts genius) in *Nihon Kobudo*.[85]

Sugino introduced several innovations into the way he taught *Tenshin Shoden Katori Shinto-ryu*, some of which created frictions with the "purists" at the *hombu dojo*. His style, for example, was influenced

by his *aikido* experience, making it appear slightly different than the "orthodox" version. He also broke with tradition, introducing the *dan* system (he apparently never used *kyu* ranks), while also retaining the traditional system of attesting to progress. This involved earning first a *mokuroku* (obtaining the catalog of the school's different techniques), then *menkyo kaiden* (indicating the technical mastery of the curriculum) and finally *kaiden gokui* or *gokui kaiden* (indicating induction into the deepest secrets of the art, accessible only for those aged 42 years or more).

Sugino had several long-term foreign students who now teach his art overseas. In 1995, at the age of 91, he traveled to France where he amazed an audience with his demonstration of *Tenshin Shoden Katori Shinto-ryu*. Sugino retired from active teaching after nearly losing an arm to a blood clot in 1995, but continued teaching and supervising his *dojo* almost until his death on June 13, 1998 at the age of 94. He left his *dojo* and style to his son, Sugino Yukihiro (杉野至寛, born 1937).

Sugino Yoshio training with his son.

SUGINO YOSHIO'S PERSONALITY

Sugino Yoshio is best known to the public for his choreography of movie fight scenes and his many demonstrations. But among those who had the privilege of training with him, his teaching style and personality are likely what is best remembered. According to various accounts by his students, Sugino was a demanding teacher, constantly seeking excellence himself and pushing his students to achieve it as well. At the same time, Sugino was a down-to-earth, friendly, and accommodating person, patient, and with a sunny disposition. He had the demeanor of an old *samurai*, which is what attracted Kurosawa and Mifune to him in the 1950s; he "wasn't the type of person to demand deep respect but he got it nonetheless."[86]

According to one of his senior foreign students, Sugino was

> very balanced in his character. By this I mean he could be strict, in a nice way. Like a school teacher, he knew what you needed. This is what you need and he would point it out. But even in doing this, he was very kind. He corrected you when it needed to be corrected.
>
> And he was very patient. He always taught with great patience and slowly gave us the proper corrections and adjustments, bit by bit. He would say "*mo ichi do*", meaning one more time. There was always one more time. I remember that he would watch us practice, watch our technique, even if it was bad or good, and he would stroke his long, white beard, in deep contemplation. He also encouraged us. He smiled a lot. And he always nodded and smiled when we gave a good effort and showed good spirit.
>
> In terms of his technique, I was always amazed by the way he moved, floating around the old tatami floor. Effortless and balanced and yet with sharp technique that took your breath away. Over the years, as my technique improved and more speed and force were added, I still never got near enough to touch him. He would just look at me and softly move away from my sword. At the end of 3-4 long forms, I was exhausted. But the old master was just smiling. He looked frail but he was still very sharp. His technique was strong but still gentle. It was effortless and his timing immaculate.

He knew two English words: "look" and "look". In other words, he taught me that you have to observe carefully. Good words! That is why we continue the practice of *"mitori geiko"*—learn by watching—in our regular practice sessions. It means when you are not on the floor, you are watching and learning. [87]

Another foreign student remembered him similarly:

I came up to the door... and knocked. The door was opened by a smiling little old man who bowed and ushered me in. Sugino *Sensei* himself. He beamed the entire time I was there, shaking my hand and bowing so often I thought my back would give out from keeping up... In all my experiences with him...he has been unfailingly kind, courteous and friendly. He treats everyone the same way he treated me: big smiles and good-natured appreciation for anyone who tries hard. I have never seen him show the slightest sign of anger or irritation, not even when I clonked him on the elbow when I mistakenly performed *yokomen* instead of *yokodo*. He just laughed and told me to try it again.[88]

The same student noted that in the Sugino *dojo,*

Everyone practises with everyone else, and the pecking order is not very carefully maintained. If the senior student training with me makes a mistake, I feel perfectly comfortable questioning him, and I welcome the questions of junior students (when I can understand them). Nobody sits exclusively in *seiza* while waiting for a turn (only two pairs can practise at once), but instead we move about the room, laugh and complain about how hot or cold it is. There are usually some children present, the grandchildren of Sugino *Sensei,* who practise but also lend a touch of comic relief here and there... I cannot emphasize enough how comfortable and fun this *dojo* is.

Sugino was also polite and respectful of other styles and teachers, unlike some masters who tend to denigrate others: "Many times after Sunday practice, we pulled out some tables and cushions from the closet and sat down for a glass of beer and some snacks. We often talked about other *ryu-ha* (styles), techniques, or other teachers, but when someone spoke of them in a not so favourable way, *O-sensei* would immediately make it clear that this kind of talk was not acceptable. He would pull his long white beard, shake his head and say: 'If you cannot talk nicely about them, change the subject'."[89]

Perhaps most characteristic of Sugino *Sensei*'s personality is the following story, related by one of his foreign students:

> The old master taught by example and knew that us watching him move and do technique was paramount to learning. I can easily recall his intense and focused eyes during practice. Observing every inch of you, carefully moving and responding.
>
> But he even knew that we watched his every reaction and his conduct. In this, he also set good examples for us to follow in our lives. He was an old man, in his late 80's, and with his false teeth, it was not easy to understand him, even to the native Japanese who did not know him well. Every now and then, when he laughed very hard or did a strong *kiai*, his teeth would come out. Sometimes they dropped onto the tatami. He would just pick them up, put them right back in and continue. After bowing off the floor, he would comb his hair back, tilt his head back and have a good laugh about it. Although he was the grandmaster, he never took himself too seriously.[90]

SUGINO YOSHIO

QUESTIONS ABOUT SUGINO'S "LEGITIMACY"

Questions have been raised, especially among the foreign practitioners of *Tenshin Shoden Katori Shinto-ryu* about the "legitimacy" of Sugino Yoshio's teachings, and especially the legitimacy of his son's accession as his successor. Some "purists" claim that only those who have sworn by *keppan* at the *honbu dojo* and have been awarded teaching licenses either by the 20th *soke*, Iizasa Yasusada, or the style's chief instructor (*shihan*), Otake Risuke (大竹利典, born 1926), can legitimately teach the style. There are several key elements to this argument.[91]

<u>Soke vs Shihan</u>. The first thing that is important to recognize is that *Tenshin Shoden Katori Shinto-ryu* is a state-registered "Important Cultural Property" which essentially "belongs" to the Iizasa family and which has one or more people registered with the state as protectors of its legacy. The *soke* (head of household) is generally the eldest son of the previous *soke*, or someone else designated by him as successor (perhaps an adopted son or son-in-law who changes his surname to Iizasa). Up until 1898, the *soke*—Iizasa Shuri-no-suke Morisada—appears simultaneously to have served as the chief instructor. Currently, the 20th *soke*, Yasusada, has variously been reported as physically unable to train or otherwise incapable of fulfilling that role. In 1968, Otake Risuke was appointed *shihan*, while Yasusada remains *soke*. Yasusada remains in charge of policy decisions; Otake in charge of instruction. Apparently either can award or recognize a teaching license in the style, but only these two are authorized to do so.

<u>A gap in succession and confusion after the 18th *soke*</u>. Some of the confusion arising about who is authorized to teach the style derives from a gap in the succession. Morisada, the 18th *soke*, died in 1898 at the age of 59 without leaving a male successor. For the next 20 years, his widow oversaw the interests of the family, but instruction was carried out by nine top experts, all between 38 and 70 years of age, including the principle instructor (*shihan*), Yamaguchi Kumajiro. The others were: Kamagata Minosuke, Tamai Kisaburo, Shiina Ichizo, Ito Tanekichi, Kuboki Sozaemon, Isobe Kouhei, Hayashi Yazaemon, and Motomiya (Hongu) Toranosuke. Sugino, of course, trained under Tamai, Kuboki, Ito, and especially Shiina.

During that period (roughly 1900-1915), there were at least 10 branch schools of *Tenshin Shoden Katori Shinto-ryu*, each teaching slightly differently and answering to or under the direction of one of the nine *sensei*.[92]

This situation left a sufficiently confusing picture, as various students learned slightly different approaches to the style from the nine *sensei*. But the confusion was deepened when Yamaguchi *Shihan* died in 1918, leaving no single authority figure. It was another 11 years (1929) before a wedding within the family brought in a son-in-law who would become the 19th *soke* and adopt the name Iizasa Shuri-no-suke Kinjiro. It must have taken some time for Kinjiro to have established his *bona fides* as an instructor and *soke*. In fact, during the 1930s, the individuals generally representing the style at the famous Imperial *Embu* were Hayashi Yazaemon and Motomiya (Hongu) Toranosuke.[93] In 1938, a major exhibition was held for a visiting group of Nazi youth from Germany. Numerous types and styles of martial arts were featured, including a demonstration of *Katori Shinto-ryu* led by Shiina, along with his students Sugino Yoshio, Yoshio's sister Kimiko, his eldest son Akio, and the eldest son from his second marriage, Shigeo.[94]

Sugino Yoshio's *bona fides*. Despite some accusations by partisans of the headquarters of the style, there is no question that Sugino Yoshio was both a highly capable and "legitimate" instructor of *Tenshin Shoden Katori Shinto-ryu*, i.e., an instructor granted permission to teach by the *soke* of the style.

- Sugino began training in 1928 and continued to train and teach at the *hombu dojo* through the end of the War, despite his many other responsibilities.
- In 1935, Sugino was one of the charter members at the establishment of the *Nihon Kobudo Shinkikai* representing *Tenshin Shoden Katori Shinto-ryu*.
- In 1940, after Sugino gave a brilliant demonstration in front of the imperial prince Nashimoto Morimasa, Kinjiro, the 19th *soke* of the *Katori Shinto-ryu*, authorized him to become a teacher. From that time, Sugino's Kawasaki *dojo* became a branch school of the style. Kinjiro encouraged Sugino to spread knowledge of the style and to write a book on the subject.[95] Sugino was also awarded *menkyo kaiden* by Kinjiro.[96]

- In 1941, Sugino wrote a book on *Tenshin Shoden Katori Shinto-ryu*. Not only did the 19th *soke* write a preface praising the book (see below), but when it was translated into German in 2013, the 20th *soke*, Yasusada, wrote a preface as well.[97]
- Clearly further demonstrating that there was no rift between Sugino and the *hombu dojo* and no question of his legitimacy was the fact that Sugino over the years continued to visit the *hombu* along with his students, was warmly welcomed, and posed for photos with the *soke* and designated *shihan*, Otake.[98]
- Sugino also reportedly took the obligatory *keppan* in 1960.[99]

Is the Sugino school still "legitimate"? The point has been made—correctly—that Sugino Yoshio's right to teach *Tenshin Shoden Katori Shinto-ryu* expired with his death. Sugino was not authorized to designate anyone else to officially teach the style. He left his *dojo* to his son,

PREFACE TO SUGINO'S 1941 TENSHIN SHODEN KATORI SHINTO-RYU BUDO KYOHAN

"...The social situation here [in Japan] no longer allows us to keep the secrets of the *Katori Shinto Ryu* doctrine within the school. Since the appearance, in the spring of 1935, of the association for the revival of martial arts in Japan, I feel guilty that I have allowed some of our founders' arts to die out, therefore, I have chosen, as a service to our nation, to show the general public, through the handling of the sabre, certain parts of *Shinto Ryu*. At the right moment, Master Sugino suggested publishing, with Mme Ito Kikue's assistance, the existing techniques in order to guide the youngest amongst us. I gave him my support and hence this book has come has come to see the light of day. It contains the wealth of the author's experiences, conveys the essential spirit of the martial, and explains in detail the *Omote Waza* techniques. It may be used as a manual for beginners or for those wishing to perfect their knowledge. Being published, at this time when, attempts are being made to popularize the martial arts, I feel certain that this book will be of service to future society. Lastly I must express my admiration for the authors and the efforts that they have made.

Signed at Katori, Mid-Autumn 1941. Iizasa Shuri no Suke Kinjiro, 19th descendant of the founder."

Sugino Yukihiro, but that in itself did not make his son a "legitimate" inheritor of the style. Much has been made of the "fact" that Yukihiro has apparently never taken the *keppan* and is not recognized as a "legitimate" teacher of *Shoden Katori Shinto-ryu*. (A distinction must be made between qualified or skillful and "legitimate." The latter comes only from approval by the *soke* or *shihan*.) Again, the situation seems more complex, and Yukihiro appears to maintain good relations with the *soke* and *hombu*.

- According to one foreign observer and eye-witness, "In 2005, Sugino Yukihiro *sensei* and his students at the Sugino *dojo*, started demonstrating at Meiji Shrine under the name *Tenshin Shoden Katori Shinto-ryu* with Iizasa Yasusada *sensei* listed as the *soke*. This raised a few eyebrows as since 2005 there have been two groups representing the same *ryuha*, the other being led by Kyoso Shigetoshi *sensei*, Otake Risuke *sensei*'s son.

  On Monday, November 3rd, 2008, after the demonstrations had finished at Meiji Shrine, I attended the *naorai* [ritual feast with Shinto offerings[100]]. Following a few speeches, a toast to mark the occasion, and a little food, the representatives of the various *ryuha* were asked to stand up and say a few words.

  When the time came, Iizasa Yasusada *sensei*, who was at a table in front of the room, stood up as did the members of the Sugino *Dojo*. Iizasa *sensei* proudly identified himself as the *soke* of *Tenshin Shoden Katori Shinto-ryu*. He then gestured towards the others standing and clearly stated in Japanese: "These are members of *Katori Shinto-ryu's* branch *dojo*: the Sugino *Dojo*."[101]

- Moreover, "some of the students of the Sugino *Dojo* have said that they have routinely visited the *soke* over the years and that their *mokuroku* have always been signed by the *soke*. As another sign of at least their current relationship, Iizasa *soke* also attended the Sugino *Dojo's* 80th Anniversary Demonstration in 2007 as well."[102]

Thus, internal (and arguably petty) politics notwithstanding, there can be little question but that Sugino Yoshio was a legitimate teacher of *Tenshin Shoden Katori Shinto-ryu* and that his son and successor is recognized as such by the current *soke*.

POSTSCRIPT

POSTSCRIPT

Sugino Yoshio, although little known outside Japan, was a major figure in the 20th century Japanese martial arts world who, toward the end of his long life, attracted a significant foreign following. Although internal politics within the *Tenshin Shoden Katori Shinto-ryu* raised questions about his "legitimacy," these questions are misguided. Not only was Sugino one of a small handful of swordsmen who helped rescue *Tenshin Shoden Katori Shinto-ryu* from near-extinction in the first half of the century, he was also a very influential figure in both the formation of Kodokan *judo* and Ueshiba Morihei's *Aikido*. To the end of his life, he remained highly respected within the broader martial arts community for his dedication, service, and effort to preserve a valuable *koryu* (ancient martial tradition), he was lauded as one of the early and important figures of both *judo* and *aikido*.

Perhaps most importantly, Sugino will be remembered by his students as a patient but demanding teacher, a technical perfectionist, and a loving mentor. To those who crossed paths with him for only a short period, he will be remembered as an open-minded, engaging, humorous, and warm personality who was always ready to share his expertise with those who showed a serious and sincere interest.

Sugino lived during a unique time, at the tail-end of the old, traditional, and secretive era of martial arts and the beginning of a new, modern, popularized era. Somehow, through the nature of his personality, his dedication, and his skill, he was able to straddle these two eras and help bring the old *koryu* into modern times. Such an era will never come again; no one else will have the opportunity he and a handful of other martial artists had to span these epochs. Nor are we likely again soon to see the combination of skill, dedication, versatility, and personality represented by *Hanshi* Sugino Yoshio (1904-1998).

NOTES

1. Tsukasa Matsuzaki, "The Last Swordsman: The Yoshio Sugino Story" from *The Aikido Journal*, partially posted at http://members.aikidojournal.com/public/the-last-swordsman-the-yoshio-sugino-story-by-tsukasa-matsuzaki/. Much of the information available in English on Sugino is from this excellent source.
2. *Ibid.*
3. On the *Butokukai*, see Christopher M. Clarke, *Saving Japan's Martial Arts*. Huntingtown, MD: Clarke's Canyon Press, 2011.
4. "Yoshio Sugino" at http://www.aikicam.com/index.php?option=com_content&task=view&id=711&Itemid=56. Matsuzaki, "The Last Swordsman" indicates, apparently in error, that Sugino began training under Shingai while in college.
5. Matsuzaki, "The Last Swordsman." Listing Shingai as a "*yodan*" is a bit misleading because ranks were very different at the time. In fact, *yodan* then was much higher than its equivalent today. As sword master and *aikido* practitioner Nakakura Kiyoshi remembered, "It was really difficult to receive the 3rd rank in those days. There were no Kendo teachers who had any *dan* in elementary schools in Kagoshima Prefecture at that time (around 1922). There were only about two policemen who had 2nd *dan* and two or three who had *shodan*. It was extremely difficult to get the 3rd *dan*." Stanley Pranin and Hideo Yamanaka, "Interview with Sword Master Kiyoshi Nakakura (1)" at http://members.aikidojournal.com/public/interview-with-swordmaster-kiyoshi-nakakura1/.
6. Donn F. Draeger, *The Martial Arts and Ways of Japan, Vol. III: Modern Bujutsu & Budo*. New York: Weatherhill, 1974, page 100.
7. Matsuzaki, "The Last Swordsman."
8. See Christopher M. Clarke, "Through Japan's Narrowest Gate: The Test for *Kendo Hachidan*." Huntingtown, MD: Clarke's Canyon Press, 2014, pages 5-11.
9. See George McCall, "A brief investigation into the SHOGO system" at http://kenshi247.net/blog/2010/01/08/a-brief-investigation-into-the-development-ofthe-shogo-system/, and George McCall, "Kendo no Kata creators" at http://kenshi247.net/blog/2011/06/13/kendo-no-kata-creators/.
10. See Kim Taylor (?), "The Sword Through the Meiji Period," in *The Iaido Newsletter* at http://www.uoguelph.ca/~kataylor/06TIN90.htm.
11. See "Tamiya Ryu Iai" at http://www.agehacho.be/TamiyaShinkenRyu.html; "Tamiya Ryu Iaijutsu" at http://www.kampaibudokai.org/Tamiya.htm; Serge Mol, *Classical Swordsmanship of Japan: A Comprehensive Guide to Kenjutsu and Iaijutsu*. NP: Eibusha, 2010, pages 211 ff.
12. Matsuzaki, "The Last Swordsman."
13. *Ibid.*
14. *Ibid.*

15. "Interview with Yoshio Sugino" in *Aiki News* #69, November 1985, at https://www.aikidojournal.com/article?articleID=368.
16. Joseph R. Svinth, "Judo: Kunisaburo Iizuka" *Journal of Combative Sport*, July 2002 at http://ejmas.com/jcs/jcsart_svinth_0702.htm.
17. Englishman E.J. Harrison quoted in *ibid*.
18. Matsuzaki, "The Last Swordsman." See also "Kunisaburo Iizuka" at http://www.judo-ch.jp/english/legend/iizuka/. I have been unable to discover the meaning of the reference to "Tenshinkan." It may refer to the Imperial Fishieries Institute of which Iizuka was said to have been "master." See "Kunisaburo Iizuka" at http://en.wikipedia.org/wiki/Kunisaburo_Iizuka. For a fuller account of Iizuka's somewhat checkered career, see John Stevens, *The Way of Judo: A Portrait of Jigoro Kano & His Students*. Boston: Shambhala, pages 143-146.
19. "Kunisaburo Iizuka" in *Kodokan Hall of Fame* at http://www.judo-ch.jp/english/legend/iizuka/. Unfortunately, Iizuka got closely involved in pre-War right-wing politics and fell out with Kano after Iizuka and a number of others called for Kano's resignation after one of Kano's sons was arrested for left-wing political sympathies. See Stevens, *op. cit.*, pages 144-145.
20. Matsuzaki, "The Last Swordsman."
21. *Ibid*.
22. See Stanley Pranin, "Interview with Minoru Mochizuki (1)," *Aiki News* #54, April 1983 at http://www.aikidojournal.com/article.php?articleID=206.
23. "Interview with Yoshio Sugino"
24. See Clarke, *Saving Japan's Martial Arts*.
25. Pranin, "Interview with Minoru Mochizuki (1)."
26. See Clarke, *Saving Japan's Martial Arts*, pages 218-225 and Stevens, *The Way of Judo: A Portrait of Jigoro Kano & His Students*, pages 148-152.
27. Stevens, *The Way of Judo*. See also Simon Keegan, "Minoru Mochizuki: The most qualified of the masters?" August 10, 2014, at http://toshujutsu.wordpress.com/2014/08/10/minoru-mochizuki-the-most-qualified-of-the-masters/ says, "Because Toku was Okinawan and was known to perform breaking demonstrations it is not too much of a stretch to think he may have taught Mochizuki Karate as well." For Steven's viewpoint, see *op. cit.*, page 152. Toku is said to have frequently visited the nearby Okinawan *karate* master Motobu Choki, raising further questions both about whether he was an ethnic Okinawan and whether he studied *katate*. See "Entrada en Honshu y difusión de su arte" on Karate-jutsu.net at http://www.karate-jutsu.net/articles.php?id=63&page=2.
28. Matsuzaki, "The Last Swordsman".
29. *Ibid*.

30. Stevens, *The Way of Judo*, page 156.
31. *Ibid*, page 158.
32. Stevens, *The Way of Judo*, page 156
33. Kodokan Judo Museum & Library, http://www.kodokan.org/e_info/index_lib.html.
34. Matsuzaki, "The Last Swordsman."
35. *Ibid*.
36. *Ibid*.
37. On the possible confusion, see, for example, T. Plavecz, *Judo Encyclopedia*, "Jiro, Nango (1876-1951)" at http://judoencyclopedia.jimdo.com/history-of-judo-by-countries/japan/ and the discussion on http://judo.forumsmotion.com/t290p15-uchida-ryohei-the-key-points-of-budo.
38. Matsuzaki, "The Last Swordsman."
39. "Interview with Yoshio Sugino" in *Aiki News* #69. I have been unable to find any additional definitive information about Kanaya.
40. Matsuzaki, "The Last Swordsman."
41. On the confusing history, see Serge Mol, *Classical Fighting Arts of Japan: A Complete Guide to Koryu Jujutsu*. Tokyo: Kodansha, 2001, pages 131 ff.
42. *Ibid*. See also "Early Years of Ohtsuka Sensei and Jujutsu" at http://www.artsrn.ualberta.ca/aoki/Karate-do/History/Otsuka-jujutsu.html. One version of *Yoshin-ryu* was the style of *jujutsu* in which Ohtsuka Hironori (大塚 博紀,1892–1982), founder of *Wado-ryu karate* had achieved *menkyo kaiden* before studying *karate* with Funakoshi Gichin.
43. Mol, *op. cit.*, page 132-3.
44. See, for example, postings on http://www.ebudo.com/archive/index.php/t48591.html.
45. Quoted in Matsuzaki, "The Last Swordsman."
46. See Clarke, *Saving Japan's Martial Arts*.
47. Kano Jigoro, *Kano Jigoro Chosakushu*. Tokyo: Gogatsu Shobo, 1984 as quoted in Muromoto, "Judo's Decisive Battle."
48. Above account repeated from Clarke, *Saving Japan's Martial Arts*, pages 128-130. The best single description of this historic contest is found in Wayne Muromoto's "Judo's Decisive Battle: The Great Tournament Between Kodokan Judo's Four Heavenly Lords and the Jujutsu Masters," in *Furyu: The Budo Journal*, Issue 3. The journal has ceased production, but the article remained available online at http://www.furyu.com/archives/issue3/judo.html. Unless otherwise noted, the following descriptions and details of the contest come from this source. See also Laszlo Able, "History of JuJitsu, Part III: Bujutsu The Meiji Period Police Competitions

[sic]," at http://www.usjjf.org/articles/JuJitsuP3.htm; "Jujitsu History" at http://www.westlord.com/jujitsu-history/; Jim Chen, M.D. and Theodore Chen, "Judo Greats Past and Present," at http://judoinfo.com/greats.htm; Kosuke Nagaki, "Randori and the Unification of Jujutsu Disciplines by the Kodokan," at http://judoinfo.com/randori1.htm; and Donn Draeger, *Modern Bujutsu and Budo*. New York: Weatherhill, 1974, pages 117-118. Kano's own version is to be found in Bruce Watson, *Judo Memoirs of Jigoro Kano*. NP: Trafford Publishing, 2008, pages 49-50.

49. "Interview with Yoshio Sugino" in *Aiki News* #69.

50. Matsuzaki, "The Last Swordsman." On Nagaoka, see also Stevens, *The Way of Judo*, pages 146-148 and *Kodokan Hall of Fame*, "Shuichi Nagaoka" at http://www.judo-ch.jp/english/legend/nagaoka/. On Mifune, see Stevens, *op. cit.*, pages 148-152; "Kyuzo Mifune" at http://www.judo-ch.jp/english/legend/mifune/; and Clarke, *Saving Japan's Martial Arts*, pages 218-227.

51. "Interview with Yoshio Sugino" in *Aiki News* #69.

52. Matsuzaki, "The Last Swordsman."

53. "Interview with Yoshio Sugino" and "Yoshio Sugino" at http://www.aikicam.com/index.php?option=com_ content&task=view&id=711&Itemid =56.

54. "Interview with Yoshio Sugino" in *Aiki News* #69.

55. See, for example, "Kishomaru Ueshiba" in Stanley Pranin, *Aikido Pioneers—Pre-War Era*. Kanagawa, Japan: Aiki News, 2010, pages 327 ff.

56. "Kiyoshi Nakakura" in Stanley Pranin, *Aikido Pioneers—Pre-War Era*. Kanagawa, Japan: Aiki News, 2010, page 180.

57. Matsuzaki, "The Last Swordsman."

58. *Ibid.*

59. See "Yoshio Sugino" in Stevens, *op. cit.*, page 161.

60. Matsuzaki, "The Last Swordsman" and "Yoshio Sugino" at http://www.aikicam.com.

61. There are conflicting accounts of the date of the formation of the style. The date of 1447 coincides with Iizasa Choisai Ienao turning 60, the age at which he entered intense spiritual and martial training. The date of 1480 would have seen Choisai in his 93rd year, but it is possible that that is the date at which he named the style. For information on the history of *Tenshin Shoden Katori Shinto-ryu*, see Mol, *Classical Swordsmanship of Japan: A Comprehensive Guide to Kenjutsu and Iaijutsu*; Draeger, *The Martial Arts and Ways of Japan, Vol. III: Modern Bujutsu & Budo*. New York: Weatherhill, 1974; Donn F. Draeger, *The Martial Arts and Ways of Japan, Vol. I: Classical Bujutsu*. New York: Weatherhill, 1973; Ellis Amdur, *Old School: Essays on Japanese Martial Traditions*. Seattle: Edgework, 2002, pages 21-46; Risuke Otake, *The Deity and the Sword:*

Katori Shinto Ryu (Three volumes). Tokyo: Minato Research & Publishing Co., 1977-1978; Risuke Otake, *Katori Shinto-ryu: Warrior Tradition*. Warren, NJ: Koryu Books, 2009; "Tenshin Shoden Katori Shinto Ryu Yuishinkai Sugino Dojo—Spain Kenkyukai" at http://katorishintoryu.es/en/school; "Introduction to Tenshinsho-den Katori Shinto Ryu" at http://tenshinsho-den-katori-shinto-ryu.org/; "Tenshin Shoden Katori Shinto ryu: The history of Katory [*sic*.] Jingu" at http://www.katori.bg/en/katori.html; "Tenshinsho-den Katori Shinto Ryu" at http:/AMMA/teishinkan.net/KEISHINKAN/Katori_Shinto_ryu.html; "Tenshin Shoden Katori Shinto Ryu: The history" at http:/AMAM/.katorishintoryj.de/; "Tenshin Shoden Katori Shinto-ryu" at http://www.akban.org/; and numerous chat room postings.

62. Otake, *The Deity and the Sword*, Volume 1, page 16.
63. His schedule is given in "Tenshin Shoden Katori Shinto Ryu: The history."
64. Otake, *The Deity and the Sword*, Volume 1, page 16.
65. Mol, Classical Swordsmanship of Japan, pages 98-99.
66. *Ibid*, page 98.
67. See, for example, William Bekink, "Brief history of Tenshin Shoden Katori Shinto Ryu" (in Dutch) at http://www.aikidojo.nl/ksr/history_nl.html.
68. See, for example, "Tenshin Shoden Katori Shinto ryu: The history of Katory [sic.] Jingu."
69. On the Katori Shrine, see for example, "Tenshin Shoden Katori Shinto Ryu: The Katori Jingu"; Japan-Guide.com, "Katori Shrine" at http://www.japan-guide.com/e/e6408.html; "Katori Shrine" at http://www.sawara-cci.or.jp/aruki/english/katori_shrine.html; and Chiba Convention Bureau and International Center, "Katori Jingu Shrine" at http://www.ccb.or.jp/e/_sightseeing/2256.
70. For further information on the convoluted and often confusing story of the ancient gods, their actions, and their religious significance, see for example, "Encyclopedia of Shinto" at http://eos.kokugakuin.ac.jp/modules/xwords/; A to Z Photo Dictionary, Japanese Buddhist Statuary, "Shinto Deities (Kami), Supernatural Animals, Creatures, and Shape Shifters" at http://www.onmarkproductions.com/html/shinto-deities.html; Sokyo Ono, *Shinto: the Kami Way*. Rutland, VT: Tuttle, 2004; Motohisa Yamakage, *The Essence of Shinto: Japan's Spiritual Heart*. New York: Kodansha, 2012; and especially *The Kojiki: Records of Ancient Matters* (Trans. Basil Hall Chamberlain). Rutland, VT: Tuttle, 1981 and *Nihongi: Chronicles of Japan from the Earliest Times to A.D. 697* (Trans. W.G. Aston). Rutland, VT: Tuttle, 1972.
71. "Tenshin Shoden Katori Shinto-ryu" at http://www.akban.org/wiki/Category:Katori_(TSKSR)_Techniques. In addition to this website, videos

of *Tenshin Shoden Katori Shinto-ryu* can be found at https://www.youtube.com/watch?v=94KIOv5gWBU. Videos of the head instructor of the style, Otake Risuke, can be seen at https://www.youtube.com/watch?v=94KIOv5gWBU; https://www.youtube.com/watch?v=on98wYpoovU; https://www.youtube. com/watch?v=xVOQwy_WH00; https://www.youtube. com/watch?v=S_s2CntRV84; and https://www.youtube.com/watch?v=J0mo4CR7qJk. A video of Sugino performing aspects of the style can be found at https://www.youtube.com/watch?v=PoBIJyWKIUY; https://www.youtube.com/watch?v=g-ys3ZIzdcs; https://www.youtube.com/watch?v=4EvjslbRTaA; https://www.youtube.com/watch?v=PoBIJyWKIUY&list= PL53DF04E3EBB77A04; and https://www.youtube.com/watch?v=0MtWtPEbTb0. A short video of the style practiced in full ancient Japanese armor can be viewed at https://www.youtube.com/watch?v=VtpB8Ir4W7o. Commercial DVDs of the style include Sugino Yoshio "Tenshin Shoden Katori Shinto Ryu" (2003) available at http://www.budovideos.com/tenshin-shoden-katori-shinto-ryu-with-yoshio-sugino-dvd.html; Nihon Kobudo series, "Katori Shinto Ryu Kenjutsu" (2003) available at http://www.budovideos.com/katori-shinto-ryu-kenjutsu-dvd-nihon-kobudo-series.html; Nori Shigemitsu, "Origin of Japanese Martial Arts: Tenshin Shoden Katori Shinto Ryu DVD 1" (2013) available at http://www.budovideos. com/origin-of-japanese-martial-arts-tenshin-shoden-katori-shinto-ryu-dvd-1-with-nori-shigemitsu.html; and Nori Shigemitsu, "Origin of Japanese Martial Arts: Tenshin Shoden Katori Shinto Ryu DVD 2" (2013) available at http://www.budovideos.com/origin-of-japanese-martial-arts-tenshin-shoden-katori-shinto-ryu-dvd-2-with-nori-shigemitsu.html. There is also an out-of-print video of Sugino performing, produced by Panther Videos entitled "Kobujutsu: Ancient Japanese Weapons Martial Art." On the *keppan* (blood oath) see, Amdur, *Old School: Essays on Japanese Martial Traditions*, pages 253-270.

72. Yoshio Sugino & Kikue Ito, "Tenshin Shoden Katori Shinto Ryu Budo Kyohan" at http://www.koryu.nl/koryu.nl/artik.b2.ENG.budo.kyohan.html.
73. Matsuzaki, "The Last Swordsman" and "Interview with Yoshio Sugino."
74. Matsuzaki, "The Last Swordsman"
75. *Ibid.*
76. *Ibid.*
77. Yoshio Sugino & Kikue Ito, "Tenshin Shoden Katori Shinto Ryu Budo Kyohan." The city of Kawasaki was struck by U.S. bombing raids several times in April 1944.
78. Matsuzaki, "The Last Swordsman."
79. *Ibid.*
80. *Ibid.*
81. See the extensive documentation in Jason Couch, (Edited, organized, in-

troduced, and transcribed by Joseph Svinth), "Documentation Regarding the Budo Ban in Japan, 1945-1950," *Journal of Combative Sport*, December 2002, found at http://ejmas.com/jcs/jcsart_svinth_1202.htm

82. Matsuzaki, "The Last Swordsman"
83. "Yoshio Sugino" at http://www.aikicam.com/index.php?option=com_content&task=view&id=711&Itemid=56. On Mori, see Richard John Bowring, *Mori Ogai and the Modernization of Japanese Culture*. Cambridge: University of Cambridge Oriental Publications, 1979.
84. Matsuzaki, "The Last Swordsman."
85. "Profile: Sugino *Sensei*." *Cutting Edge: A Publication for all Things Related to Iaido, Iaijutsu and Kenjustu*. (Online magazine.) Issue 5, July 2014, page 16.
86. On the IMAF, which was established in 1952, see "International Martial Arts Federation" at http://en.wikipedia.org/wiki/International_Martial_Arts_Federation.
87. "One on One with Sazen Larsen Kusano Sensei (Sugino branch, Katori Shinto Ryu), Part One: About Yoshio Sugino Sensei," in *The Iaido Journal*, September 2008, at http://ejmas.com/tin/2008tin/tinnart_long_0810sazan11.html.
88. *Ibid.*
89. Corey Reid, "Sugino Dojo: Studying Katori Shinto Ryu in Japan," *The Iaido Newsletter,* 1998, reprinted 2006 at http://ejmas.com/tin/tinframe.htm.
90. "One on One with Sazen Larsen Kusano Sensei."
91. *Ibid.*
92. Much of the information on the controversies over the Sugino *dojo*'s "legitimacy" is found in web postings. For background on the controversy and the hiatus in succession, see for example, Yoshio Sugino & Kikue Ito, "Tenshin Shoden Katori Shinto Ryu Budo Kyohan" at http://www.koryu.nl/koryu.nl/artik.b2.ENG.budo.kyo-han.html; "Tenshin ryu vs Muso Jikiden Eishin ryu…" on "Martial Arts Planet" at http://martialartsplanet.com/forums/showthread.php?t=101485; "Tenshin Shoden Katori Shinto Ryu Yuishinkai Sugino Dojo—Spain Kenkyukai" at http://katorishintoryu.es/en/school; "Katori Ryu Question" at http://www.e-budo.com/archive/index.php/t-25595.html; "Tenshin shoden Katori Shinto Ryu" on "swordforum" at http://www.swordforum.com/forums/show-thread.php?93308-Tenshin-shoden-Katori-Shinto-Ryu; "Tenshin Shoden Katori Shinto Ryu" at http://kiaiaikibudo.plessis.free.fr/tenshin_shoden_katori_shinto_ryu_3657.htm (in French); "Katori shinto ryu Jean Prieur et Pierre Rousseau" at https://www.youtube.com/all_comments?v=iwR1JeIeJEo&lc=kP2vTqdbhkiM8n ArqmhSgI9PiYtxN2RN5V66D4U5BMo (partly in French); "Talk:Tenshin Shoden Katori Shinto-ryo/Archive 1" at http://www.territorioscuola.com/wikipedia/en.wikipedia.php?title=Talk:

Tenshin_Sh%C5%8Dden_ Katori_Shint%C5%8D-ry%C5%AB/ Archive_1; and Simone Chierchini, "Storia Moderna del Katori Shinto Ryu: Una Panoramica" (in Italian, "Modern History of the Katori Shinto Ryu: An Overview") at http://aikidoitalia.com/2013/11/23/storia-moderna-del-katori-shinto-ryu-una-panoramica/.

93. Simone Chierchini, "Storia Moderna del Katori Shinto Ryu: Una Panoramica."
94. *Ibid.* See also https://www.youtube.com/watch?v=XiqcmntUi-8, a rare video of the two apparently from a 1931 *embu*.
95. Simone Chierchini, "Storia Moderna del Katori Shinto Ryu: Una Panoramica."
96. See, for example, Yoshio Sugino & Kikue Ito, "Tenshin Shoden Katori Shinto Ryu Budo Kyohan"; "Tenshin Shoden Katori Shinto Ryu Yuishinkai Sugino Dojo—Spain Kenkyukai"; "Katori Ryu Question" at http://www.e-budo.com/archive/index.php/t-25595.html; and Matsuzaki, "The Last Swordsman."
97. It is not clear if Sugino ever received the highest title of "*gokui kaiden*," signifying introduction to all the secrets of the art. Many of these "secrets" appear to have to do with religious and esoteric knowledge, something Sugino appears not to have heavily emphasized in his teaching.
98. Preface from "Katori Ryu Question" at http://www.e-budo.com/archive/index.php/t-25595.html but widely available elsewhere as well.
99. See, for example, "Talk:Tenshin Shoden Katori Shinto-ryo/Archive 1" at http://www.territorioscuola.com/wikipedia/en.wikipedia.php?title=Talk:Tenshin_Sh%C5%8Dden_ Katori_Shint%C5%8D-ry%C5%AB/Archive_1, based on first-hand accounts.
100. *Ibid.*
101. See "Naorai" at http://eos.kokugakuin.ac.jp/modules/xwords/entry.php?entryID=768.
102. "Tenshin shoden Katori Shinto Ryu" on "swordforum" at http://www.swordforum.com/forums/showthread.php?93308-Tenshin-shoden-Katori-Shinto-Ryu. For a similar statement, see "Tenshin ryu vs Muso Jikiden Eishin ryu…" on "Martial Arts Planet" at http://martialartsplanet.com/forums/showthread.php?t=101485.
103. "Tenshin shoden Katori Shinto Ryu" on "swordforum," *op. cit.*

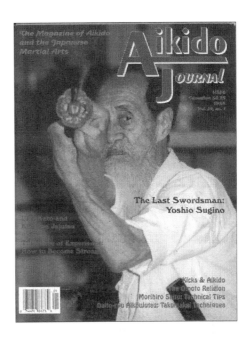

OTHER BOOKS BY THE AUTHOR

All available at www.Amazon.com.

EMPTY-HANDED I ENTERED THE WORLD: GREAT OKINAWAN KARATE MASTERS LOST IN 2012-2014. *Empty-handed I Entered the World* consists of brief biographies of more than a dozen senior Okinawan *karate* masters who have died between mid-2012 and mid-2014. Within the next few years, this entire cohort will be gone. Those who have passed from the scene run the gamut of styles and former teachers, including masters of various branches of *Shorin-ryu, Goju-ryu, Uechi-ryu, Kempo,* and *Motobu-ryu*. As these pre-War-trained masters die off, we are losing not only vital links to the past but a vast storehouse of knowledge. The challenge in the future for serious foreign martial artists training under top-notch instructors in their home countries will be to identify the best of the best in Okinawa and to make the trade-offs in cost, time, devotion and loyalty, and conflicting instruction to break through the natural barriers that prevent many Asian instructors from teaching the best they have to offer. Fortunately, in the globalized world of the early 21st century, there are organizations that help non-Okinawan *karateka* make connections and arrange training periods with some of the best masters on the island. In the current information age, there is also an abundant flow of information about available training opportunities and assessments of various instructors and schools. In addition, many foreign instructors (and a few Okinawans and Japanese) are not only working hard to preserve "traditional" *karate*, but to advance our knowledge of how to apply its time-honored wisdom in the modern age. All this suggests that despite the popularity of MMA and the pessimism of some that the days of "traditional" *karate* are numbered, the future is actually bright. For those willing to dedicate the time and effort, the opportunities to learn are better than they have ever been. 104 pages, August 2014, $8.06.

MODERN-DAY SAMURAI: KOTAKA SUKESABURO MINAMOTO-NO SADAYASU SADAO - AN APPRECIATION AND HISTORY OF HIS KENJUTSU STYLE. *Modern-day Samurai* tells the story of a modern sword master, Dr. Kotaka Sadao (1933-2013), who learned from one of the last true *samurai*, a member of the famous *Shinsengumi* of the 1860s. The book relates the life of Dr. Kotaka, his numerous and remarkable exploits as a swordsman, the history of his style going back for hundreds of years, and story of the turbulent times during which his teacher learned and actually utilized this style of swordsmanship. Full of wit and wisdom, the book is heavily illustrated with maps, charts, and many never-before-published photos. Extensively documented, it also provides a complete bibliography for those wanting to learn more about *Kendo* or Japanese history. A must read for anyone interested in the Japanese martial arts, the Meiji Restoration, or the history of the *Shinsengumi* or the *samurai*. **Five-star rated.** one reader said "As one of the last-surviving senior students who studied directly under Kotaka Sukesaburo Minamoto-no Sadayasu Sadao, I wish to express my heartfelt appreciation to Mr. Clarke for his detailed and meticulous research. Indeed, the description above does not do justice to the author's success at piecing together historical documents, collecting personal letters and photographs from Dr. Kotaka's wife as well as from many of his former students, and placing all of this information into historical context... Mr. Clarke's memorial volume is a storehouse of information about the development of *kendo* and the *Itto-ryu*, about the *Shinsengumi*, and—even more important—about how all of 'that' was transplanted to the New World by way of a particular person (Kotaka-sensei) who gives a face to a story that would otherwise get bogged down in information overload." 222 pages, July 2014, $10.76.

OKINAWAN KARATE: A HISTORY OF STYLES AND MASTERS, VOLUME 1: SHURI-TE AND SHORIN-RYU. *Okinawan Karate: A History of Styles and Masters, Volume 1: Shuri-te and Shorin-ryu* is the most comprehensive and complete book available on the origins of Okinawan *Shuri-te* and *Shorin-ryu karate*, with descriptions of the various branches, detailed biographies of the major Okinawan *Shuri-te/Shorin-ryu* masters from ancient times to today, analytical assessments of some of their accomplishments, and numerous photos and illustrations. This book is a "must-have" for all serious martial arts students. A near-**five-star rating on Amazon.com**. Reviewer Kevin Meisner said "This book has become one of my favorites on Shuri-te history. As a student for the past 30+ years, I thoroughly enjoyed the tour, including pictures I had not seen before, stories I had not heard before, and even connections I had not made before. I have been able to use the 'new' information to follow up with internet searches, finding even more great information and even video footage of some of the historical figures (Chibana Chosin *Passai*). Thank you for writing such an interesting book, looking forward to Volume 2 and more." "Shooter 16a2" opined "This book is helping me with my research. It not only gives the histories of past Masters but, also has a few very old pictures of a few. I must have for the serious Okinawan *karate-ka*." B. Ballardini enthused, "A Great Reference Book. A must have for all the researchers in ancient karate. A complete view on the most precious Okinawan schools and their heritage." 376 pages, August 24, 2012, $19.95.

OKINAWAN KARATE: A HISTORY OF STYLES AND MASTERS, VOLUME 2: FUJIAN ANTECEDENTS, NAHA-TE, GOJU-RYU AND OTHER STYLES. *Okinawan Karate: A History of Styles and Masters, Volume 2: Fujian Antecedents, Naha-te, Goju-ryu and Other Styles* is the most comprehensive and complete book available on the origins of the Okinawan *karate* styles that emerged from the Fujian Southern Shaolin boxing styles. It contains a thorough historical description of the Ryukyu kingdom's relations with both China and Japan; the background of the Fujian Southern Shaolin Temple and the various styles of Chinese martial arts that emerged from that lineage; the influence of Fujian boxing on the two great *Naha-te* styles of *Goju-ryu* and *Uechi-ryu* as well as the history of those styles and their major branches and masters; and the histories of *Isshin-ryu, Kojo-ryu, Ryuei-ryu,* and *Motobu Udundi (Gotente)*. In each case, the book provides analytical assessments of the style's characteristics, descriptions of their curricula, and critical assessments of the accomplishments and controversies surrounding some of their great masters. This book is lavishly illustrated with photos, art work, maps, tables and charts, including a detailed description of the social and court ranks of the Ryukyu kingdom. Its footnotes provide access to a wide array of sources in English, Chinese, and Japanese--including available videos on the styles and masters--for those who wish to learn more. **A five-star rating on Amazon.com**. Reviewer B. Ballardini says "A must have for all the researchers in ancient karate. A complete view on the origins of the Okinawan schools." Reviewer Earle Barrell comments "This book should be in the possession of every *Goju* teacher in the world. It is well researched and documented with footnotes. Has reference to just about every article and book ever written on *Goju* and *Naha-te* style *karate*. For 40 Years I have read everything I could get my hands on about *Goju* history and this is by far the most complete history in terms of combining all the known research in the English and Japanese languages. It will help you understand the true *karate* and how it developed. You will not be disappointed." 376 pages, August 24, 2012, $19.95.

OKINAWAN KOBUDO: A HISTORY OF WEAPONRY STYLES AND MASTERS. *Okinawan Kobudo: A History of Weaponry Styles and Masters* is a comprehensive and complete book on the origins of the Okinawan kobudo (weaponry). It contains a description of the early history of weaponry in the Ryukyus; the relationship of *kobudo* to *karate*; and several myths and misunderstandings about Okinawan weaponry. In addition to profiles of nearly a dozen ancient *kobudo* masters, this book includes detailed histories and analysis of the major lineages/styles of *kobudo*, including the Yabiku-Taira, Yamane, Matayoshi, Ufuchiku, and Motobu Udundi (Gotente) schools of *kobudo*. In each case, the book provides a history of the masters—from the founders to today's masters—analytical assessments of the style's characteristics, descriptions of their curricula, and lineage charts. It contains chapters on each of the weapons of *Ryukyu kobudo*, including extensive bibliographies on where to find more information about each. The book is lavishly illustrated with photos, art work, maps, tables and charts, including a detailed table of all the major recognized *kata* for each weapon in *Ryukyu kobudo*. Its footnotes provide access to a wide array of sources in English, French, German, Spanish, and Japanese—including available videos on the styles and masters—for those who wish to learn more. As the companion to the author's two volume, five-star rated *Okinawan Karate: A History of Styles and Masters*, this book is an absolute "must-have" for all serious martial arts students. Rated **five stars** on Amazon.com, it has been called "**An Excellent, well researched and informative book**," Fantastic," and the "**Most Comprehensive History of Okinawan Kobujutsu.**" 392 pages, July 2013, $16.71.

RAMBLINGS FROM A TEN FOOT SQUARE HUT: REFLECTIONS AFTER 50 YEARS IN THE MARTIAL ARTS. What is a "martial art"? Are we practicing an "art," which by definition is a means of self-expression without the need for any practical application or self-justification? Or are we practicing a "martial" discipline, something that requires effective training in combative technique, that prepares us to defend ourselves, perhaps even to take another person's life or lose our own in self-defense or in the effort to defend our loved ones or our principles? What relationship does our "modern" "martial art" bear to the old *samurai* way of life, the way of Bushido, the way of the warrior? What should we expect of our "martial arts"—and of ourselves? Related to this, how did we get from the highly practical original Okinawan "*te*" to the often stylized, unrealistic, and competitive "*karatedo*" we practice today? Does our modern *karatedo* provide realistic methods for confronting the kinds of self-defense and combative situations we face in the 21st century? If not, did something get lost in the transmission from the 17th and 18th century to the 21st? The popularization of Mixed Martial Arts (MMA) since the 1990s has reinforced this dilemma for practitioners of such "classical" martial arts as *karatedo*. Why do our traditional methods not prepare us for grappling or fighting from the floor? Why did classical *karate* practitioners keep losing to grapplers? Do we need to drop our traditional *karatedo* and take up MMA to find an effective self-defense or fighting system for the 21st century? These questions bedevil those of us who love and cling to our "traditional" martial arts. This books carefully examines how we arrived at this situation, how various experts have thought about it and attempted to find answers to our dilemma, and provides a sensible, workable set of principles that show that traditional martial arts are not obsolete, that they contain a wide range of effective combative strategies, tactics, and techniques that are just as usable today as they were when they were assembled into "*kata*", or forms for helping the student remember and practice realistic self-defense and combat while alone. For those wrestling with how to make their *karate* "work," this is a must-have book. Don't flounder or lose faith. And don't ignore the problem. Buy this book and start to discover your own answers to how to make your *karate* effective.

Five-star rated. Practical *karate* pioneer Iain Abernethy says "I dived straight in. I got nothing else done that day! The author's knowledge and passion for *bunkai* makes this book an enjoyable and informative page-turner. What I really liked about the book is that it draws together many sources from the past and present. Unlike any book I've read on *kata* application before, this book not only brings together information from the past, it also looks at many of the contemporary approaches to *bunkai* and their proponents. I was honoured to feature in this, and just in case you think this is a bit of "mutual back slapping", let me assure you the author's critique of my work is not without criticism. The reason I've written this review is because it's a great book which has much to add to the modern conversation around *bunkai*. The book is concise without being shallow; a difficult thing to pull off. Every page has valuable information and the author does a great job of guiding the reader through it all. The author also manages to strike the balance between giving his own views on the source material, and yet never letting his views obscure the nature of that material. It truly is a superb read which is very information rich. This is a book that all *karateka* with an interest in *kata* application need to read. In a word: Excellent!" 208 pages, July 2013, $13.38.

SAVING JAPAN'S MARTIAL ARTS. *Saving Japan's Martial Arts* is the story of how a young school teacher helped spark a martial arts revolution in Japan, rescue Japan's ancient martial arts from the brink of oblivion, built Japan's Olympic Movement, and became a driving force behind modern education in Japan. It is the only comprehensive biography in English of the remarkable Jigoro Kano (1860-1938), founder of *Kodokan Judo*. *Saving Japan's Martial Arts* also contains biographical sketches of more than a dozen top *Judo* students including Maeda Mitsuyo, who taught *Judo* and *Jujutsu* to the Gracies in Brazil; Yamashita Yoshiaki, who taught President Theodore Roosevelt *Judo* in the White House; Shoriki Matsutaro, *Judo* master, founder of the Yomiuri media empire, creator of professional baseball in Japan, and Japan's first nuclear energy commissioner; and many others. *Saving Japan's Martial Arts* contains a detailed history of the bloody end of the Tokugawa shogunate, including the political struggles, assassinations and duels, and battles portrayed in the blockbuster 2003 Tom Cruise movie, "The Last Samurai."

Saving Japan's Martial Arts is chock-full of rare, vintage pictures and descriptions of the training and masters of the ancient Japanese martial arts. It should be required reading for anyone interested in the development of the Asian martial arts and for those who want to understand how those arts survived one of the most tumultuous centuries in Japanese history, a century that saw Japan emerge from an isolated and backward feudal autocracy to a modernized, industrialized major power. **A five-star rating on Amazon.com.** Reviewer Ty Freeland says "I been studying the martial arts for thirty one years and I have always been fascinated not only with the physical techniques of the arts but with their history as well. I know quite a bit about the history of most martial arts but *judo* was one that I never really bothered to research extensively. I knew the basic history and origin of the art but always wanted a more thorough understanding of how it came about. This book educated me very nicely. If you wish to know the who, what, when where and why of the art of *judo* and get to know the founder of the art then look no further. This book is for you. *Saving Japan's Martial Arts* is an excellent book that gives detailed information on the history and very nature of *judo*. Why its different from its parent art of *jujutsu*, how Jigoro Kano developed the art and his long journey in establishing the art across the world. I absolutely loved this book. If you're interested in *judo* or its founder then this book will make an excellent addition to your library. Happy reading." 284 pages, October 2011, $16.95.

SAMURAI, SCOUNDRELS, AND SAINTS: STORIES FROM THE MARTIAL ARTS. Asian history is replete with stories of combat, heroism, self-sacrifice, valor, strategy, and compassion. *Samurai, Scoundrels, and Saints* includes more than three dozen such stories, ranging from the famous woman warrior, Tomoe Gozen, to how the renowned *samurai*, Miyamoto Musashi was almost killed in the bath tub, and from the monk who defied the Mongols, to the supernatural creatures that reputedly taught the famous warrior Yoshitsune how to fight. It includes tales of daring rescues, narrow escapes, treachery, and Zen enlightenment. The final tale tells the story of "The Last *Samurai*" who remained in the jungle of Guam from the time of the Japanese surrender in 1945 until he was finally convinced the war was over and he could surrender in 1972. *Samurai, Scoundrels and Saints* is heavily illustrated and has a beautiful full-color cover. It is sure to appeal to martial artists, arm-chair enthusiasts, those interested in Asian history, and people just looking for a "good read." Reviewer mrktw said "This book and its companion volume, *Warriors and Wisemen*, occupy a place of honor on my martial arts bookshelf next to *O-Sensei* Richard Kim's, *The Classical Man* and *The Weaponless Warriors*. Like *Sensei* Kim, Dr. Clarke collects stories that draw from rich martial arts traditions that developed over many centuries in many countries...The stories have been drawn from many primary and secondary sources -- the bibliography lists over a hundred articles and books. This book is a reflection of [his] deep knowledge and understanding." 214 pages, April 2011, $19.95.

WARRIORS AND WISEMEN: MORE STORIES FROM THE MARTIAL ARTS. The sequel to *Samurai, Scoundrels, and Saints*, *Warriors and Wisemen* tells dozens of stories from the rich martial lore of Asia ranging from the historical to the mythical, interspersed with "Zen Interludes." Lavishly illustrated, *Warriors and Wisemen* contains numerous charts and maps to make it easier to follow the action and includes extensive notes and bibliography. Enjoy such wonderful tales as the transmission of the light of Buddhahood to the Sixth Patriarch of Zen, an illiterate woodcutter; the first major rebellion against the Japanese emperor; *samurai* who later became spirits who continue to haunt Japan today; one-on-one combat between some of Japan's most famous martial artists; the life and legends of *Taiji* founder Yang Luchan's sons; the fearless warrior who tried to assassinate China's first emperor; the legendary *samurai* archer, Tametomo, who may have founded the royal house of Okinawa after losing a war and being banished; and much more. If you like rollicking stories of warriors' daring-do told within an accurate historical context, tales of great Zen masters, and legends of *samurai* who never die, you'll love this book. **Five-star rated on Amazon.com.** Reviewer mrktw enthused "Like *Samurai, Scoundrels and Saints*, this book is meticulously researched (eighty reference sources, and over one hundred endnotes) and written in a non-scholarly style that will be accessible to all readers. But as highly as I recommend *Samurai*, I believe that this book has a warmth and richness of emotion that surpasses the first volume's. In addition, this time around Dr. Clarke has provided more background for the stories, as well as 'family trees' for Zen and tai chi traditions that aid greatly in appreciating the stories. This collection is an utter delight to read, savor, and re-read." 242 pages, May 2011, $19.95.

KAMIKAZE!: JAPAN'S "DIVINE WIND" AND THE SPIRIT OF THE MARTIAL ARTS. *Kamikaze!* is the story of two wars. During the Mongol invasion of Japan in the late 1200's, the badly out-matched Japanese were saved from defeat by a fortuitous typhoon which wrecked the Mongol fleet and caused them to withdraw. The grateful Japanese called this storm the *kamikaze*, or divine wind. Japanese soldiers were to revive that name during the waning days of World War II, when they embarked on a last-ditch effort to use suicide attacks to stave off defeat. In addition to historical narratives of both wars, *Kamikaze!* includes rare Japanese woodblock prints of *samurai*, several maps, photos of the suicide vehicles used by the Japanese, and actual combat photos of American ships under attack by *kamikaze* suicide pilots. It contains excerpts from letters sent home by *kamikaze* pilots just before they embarked on their final missions and an extensive list for further reading. 74 pages, April 2011, $12.95.

FATHER FROG: ASIAN STORIES AND ACTIVITIES FOR YOUNGSTERS. *Father Frog* is a charming collection of Asian folk stories and tales for youngsters from five to fifteen, told by old Father Frog. Each story has a moral about good behavior and character. The book is lavishly illustrated with classical Japanese art, original brush paintings by the author, and other delightful illustrations. It contains numerous activities for children ranging from "word find" and "word scramble" puzzles to mazes, coloring, and image matching that will appeal to children of all ages from five and up. This book is a great way for teachers and parents to introduce their children to aspects of traditional Japanese and Chinese society and folklore. Whether you read it to them or they can read it themselves, kids will love it. 146 pages, October 2012, $11.66.

Made in the USA
Lexington, KY
09 February 2017